Final 76 & 77
Roots & 1st inversions

PianoLab

G B D F A

231

❖ PianoLab

An Introduction to Class Piano

Second Edition

Carolynn A. Lindeman
San Francisco State University

250
252
246

Wadsworth Publishing Company
Belmont, California
A Division of Wadsworth, Inc.

Other books by Carolynn A. Lindeman

MusicLab: An Introduction to the Fundamentals of Music, by Carolynn A. Lindeman and Patricia Hackett (Wadsworth Publishing Company)

The Musical Classroom: Backgrounds, Models, and Skills for Elementary Teaching, Second Edition, by Patricia Hackett and Carolynn A. Lindeman (Prentice-Hall)

Women Composers of Ragtime, compiled and introduced by Carolynn A. Lindeman (Theodore Presser)

Editor: Suzanna Brabant
Editorial Assistant: Laurie Wiegler
Production Editor: Deborah Cogan
Managing Designers: James Chadwick and Cindy Schultz
Print Buyer: Martha Branch
Permissions Editor: Robert Kauser
Text Designer: Detta Penna
Copy Editor: Carole Crouse
Compositor: A-R Editions
Cover Designers: James Chadwick and Cindy Schultz
Cover Illustrator: Mark Stearney

Printed in the United States of America   49

    4 5 6 7 8 9 10—95 94

Library of Congress Cataloging-in-Publication Data

Lindeman, Carolynn A., date.
    PianoLab / Carolynn A. Lindeman. — 2nd ed.
       p.   cm.
    Includes bibliographical references (p.   ) and index.
    ISBN 0-534-13944-2
    1. Piano—Methods—Group instruction.   2. Music—Theory,
    Elementary.   3. Piano music.   I. Title.
    MT222.L695   1991
    786.2'193—dc20   90-12677

❖ Contents

❖ **Chapter Three   44**

❖ Chapter Five   79

❖ Chapter Six   97

❖ Chapter Nine 167

❖ Supplementary Music 225

Supplementary Blues, Boogie, and Ragtime 247

Supplementary Songs with Accompaniments 253

Supplementary Songs (Melodies Only) 262

❖ Appendixes 295

❖ Preface

PianoLab, Second Edition, like the edition that preceded it, was created mindful of the challenges faced by students and their instructors in most class piano courses. Students want to play the piano as quickly as possible and often become frustrated when their physical skills do not keep pace with their conceptual skills. Their varying backgrounds, motivation, and cognitive and psychomotor skills make it impossible for everyone to learn at the same rate. Even with the best facilities, the instructor faces a limited time frame in which to teach the piano basics. It may take one or two quarters or semesters for students to learn their "keyboard geography" and become comfortable at the piano. Add to that the desire to give students more than just a brush with music concepts, and there is indeed a great deal to accomplish in a short time.

These challenges, however, are not insurmountable. Assuming that students have no prior background in music, *PianoLab*, Second Edition, focuses on teaching them to *perform*. And it goes a step further; It gives students an *understanding* of music that they can take with them, regardless of whether they continue to play the piano. Each chapter includes brief materials to develop understanding of the elements of music: melody, rhythm, harmony, and form. Students are then encouraged to apply that knowledge through performance, analysis, improvisation, transposition, harmonization, and composition.

Organization of the Book

The main focus of each chapter is the development of skills and technique. Chapter 1 invites students to explore the keyboard by *making music and creating music* before learning to read it. Subsequent chapters build on that initial exploration through the following:

A wide variety of *playing materials* (over 150), representing art music of the eighteenth through the twentieth centuries by male and female composers, indeterminate music, folk songs, piano blues, boogie-woogie, ragtime, and popular music.

Careful *grading of selections* from the simplest to the more challenging.

Development of music-reading and playing skills simultaneously through exercises and playing materials.

Composing and improvising projects to encourage and develop creativity.

Ensemble pieces (over 20) for two or more players in a number of styles, all adapted and labeled for several uses.

Technique exercises covering skills encountered within each chapter and those to come in subsequent chapters.

End-of-chapter evaluations for students and instructors to evaluate skill development and progress in musical understanding before moving ahead to the next chapter.

Additional Features

PianoLab, Second Edition, also includes a Supplementary Music section with more than fifty selections of solo classical piano pieces; blues, boogie, and ragtime; traditional folk and patriotic songs with piano accompaniment; and folk and popular melodies.

Although all the ensemble pieces are presented within the ten chapters, they are also reprinted in a special, easy-to-read section following the Supplementary Music section. There the pieces are arranged with Piano 1 and Piano 2 parts printed on the same page or with parts printed on adjacent pages.

Several appendixes on such topics as musical terms and signs, fingerings for major and minor scales, primary chords in root position and in I–IV$_4^6$–V$_5^6$ position, accompaniment patterns, information on electronic keyboards, a Timeline of Western Art Music and History, a Timeline of Selected Keyboard Composers and Keyboard Instruments, and Biographical Sketches of *PianoLab* Composers, all help to answer student questions and provide references for study, practice, and review. Following the appendixes is a Glossary of musical terms.

In addition to the subject index, *PianoLab*, Second Edition, has several specialized indexes to provide flexibility and ease of use.

PianoLab stresses strong student orientation, from the Note to Students through each chapter, where a variety of music is offered to help students acquire needed skills and concepts.

An authentic presentation of eighteenth- through twentieth-century music is an important feature of the text. Selections appear in original (*urtext*) edition with only fingerings added. Since few dynamic, tempo, or articulation markings were included in eighteenth-century music, performance notes are often provided (or occasional markings are placed in parentheses), but no editing is added by the author.

Root-position chords are introduced before chord inversions to solidify student understanding of chord building. Although only the primary chords (in root position and all inversions) are stressed, several examples in the Supplementary Songs sections include secondary chords (also, Appendix F identifies primary and secondary chords in major and minor keys).

Acknowledgments

Creating the second edition of *PianoLab* required the help and support of many people. I am particularly grateful to:

My colleagues in the San Francisco State University Music Department—Patricia Hackett, Warren Rasmussen, Alexander Post, Helen Bedesem, Eric Tamm, and the late James Harris—for their help in developing, improving, and critiquing *PianoLab* in its various stages.

Composers and friends Herbert Bielawa, Nancy Van de Vate, and Emma Lou Diemer for creating pieces especially for *PianoLab*.

Keyboard and performance practices specialist Sandra Soderlund for her critical assessment and review of the Technique Exercises and musical examples and her expert advice on eighteenth-century keyboard performance practices.

Serra High School music instructor James Jordan for his help in preparing the Biographical Sketches of *PianoLab* Composers and the information on electronic keyboards.

San Francisco State University music major Judy Fendell for her research and assistance in preparing the Timeline of Selected Keyboard Composers and Keyboard Instruments.

The following reviewers for their thoughtful and critical comments: Thomas J. Anderson, DeKalb Community College; Martha J. Baker, California State University, Fullerton; Elizabeth Barkley, Foothill College; Alice Bartels, Moorhead State University; Russell A. Bliss, Nassau Community College; Leaine Gibson, California State University, Long Beach; Margo Halsted, University of California, Riverside; Brent Heisinger, San Jose State University; Joan Kerfoot, Cosumnes River College; Dennie McGreer, Indiana University; Linda Mankin, Foothill College; Madeline Mueller, City College of San Francisco; June Nelson, El Camino College; Ronald E. Regal, Ithaca College; Dan Stehman, Los Angeles Valley College; Mary Louise Reilly, California State University, Northridge; Nancy J. Stephenson, University of Houston; Janice Trilck, University of California, Santa Barbara; and James P. Witt, San Diego City College.

Finally, my husband, Al, and son, David, for their love, understanding, and help in making *PianoLab* become a reality.

❖ Note to Students

About the Book

PianoLab, Second Edition, is designed for you, the beginning student. It assumes no background in music but does assume you have a genuine interest in learning to play the piano and learning about music. As you learn to read and play, you will discover that reading notes and playing scales and chord progressions are not enough. You must also develop an understanding of how music is put together, how it "works," and how rhythm, melody, and harmony interrelate to form musical compositions. This musical understanding evolves mainly through performance but also through analysis, improvisation, transposition, harmonization, and composition. Helping you develop these keyboard skills and music concepts is the goal of *PianoLab*.

Although *PianoLab*, Second Edition, includes more than 200 pieces of music, you do not need to learn all the music to acquire essential concepts and skills. Each chapter includes a number of musical examples for you to perform. Study several of these pieces and use the others, if you wish, for sightreading and extra practice.

Over twenty of the musical selections are arranged to be played in ensembles. The ensemble pieces may be performed with one or two students per piano or with students playing one part and the instructor the other. Parts can also be divided and doubled among students. For individual practice, you can record one part or use a tape recording of the part, then perform the other with the recording.

As you explore the playing examples in the text, you will find that music of all styles and eras, from classical music of the eighteenth through twentieth centuries to popular music, is included. All the music in *PianoLab*, Second Edition, is presented in original form. In the case of eighteenth-century music, this means that only pitches and rhythm are notated; eighteenth-century composers included few tempo, dynamic, and articulation markings in their manuscripts. Since only fingerings have been added to the eighteenth-century pieces, a few performance guidelines to remember for many pieces are these: Play *non legato* (not connected), *mezzo forte* (medium loud), and *moderato* (moderate tempo).

All musical terms and signs, such as *legato, mezzo forte,* and *moderato,* are presented in Appendix A, and information about the composers is contained in the Biographical Sketches of *PianoLab* Composers. In addition, you can place the composers and their music in the appropriate historical period by utilizing the Timeline of Western Art Music and History and the Timeline of Selected Keyboard Composers and Keyboard Instruments.

Suggestions for Practice

Certainly every beginning pianist needs to devote time outside of class to practice in order to progress and to develop skills. Reserve a particular time each day for this purpose. (A little work each day is better than a longer practice session a couple of days a week.) Here are some suggestions for your practice session:

1. Begin with several Technique Exercises. The Technique Exercises at the end of each chapter are simple patterns that can be memorized so you can direct all your attention to seeing and feeling the correct hand and finger positions and listening for good tone production.

2. Visually analyze each piece before playing to get a "picture" of the piece. Look to see how fast or how slowly the piece should be performed. Are there any changes in louds and softs? Does the piece break into easily recognizable parts? Notice how the melody moves up and down and repeats. Check the meter signature, the kinds of notes and rests, and any particular rhythmic patterns. Are chords outlined in the right- and left-hand parts? Look up all tempo and dynamic terms in Appendix A. Check information on the composer and his or her place in history in the Biographical Sketches of *PianoLab* Composers and the two timelines.

3. Practice new and old pieces in several different ways. Review the keyboard position(s). Perform just the rhythm of the piece. Perform the piece slowly hands together, listening carefully. Practice hands separately, in small sections, and so on. Always evaluate your playing. Practice problem spots slowly. Repeat until you are satisfied with your performance.

4. End your practice session by improvising a bit at the keyboard. Create music using ideas and composing projects found in the chapters or by applying your own ideas.

Class Piano and You

As you study the piano in a group setting, you will find that beginning pianists progress at different rates of speed. Some in your class will develop eye and hand coordination quickly and almost effortlessly. Others will work diligently and slowly to achieve the same results in a much longer period of time. These individual differences are always present in the mastery of a new technical skill, whether it be sports or piano playing. However, although beginning pianists develop the physical skills at different rates, most adults develop music concepts at a similar rate. Be aware that your physical and conceptual skills may not keep pace with each other. Try to understand this phenomenon and do not become frustrated by it. Most of all, your progress and pleasure in piano study depend on you. You must make the personal commitment and accept the challenge of learning a new skill. It is hoped that *PianoLab*, Second Edition, and the music course in which you are enrolled will help you meet those challenges and "turn you on" to the exciting world of music.

❖ Introduction

The Piano

Historical Development

Piano, pianoforte. A stringed instrument whose strings are struck by hammers activated by keys, and which, since the end of the 18th century, has been the principal domestic keyboard instrument in Europe and America.*

Bartolommeo Cristofori is credited with inventing the piano about 1709 in Florence, Italy. The piano differed from the earlier keyboard instruments, the clavichord and the harpsichord, in that its hammer action could provide continuous gradations of loud and soft tones. Cristofori's name for his invention was *gravicembalo col piano e forte* ("harpsichord with soft and loud"). The instrument, however, came to be known as the *pianoforte* or the abbreviated name *piano*. (A Timeline of Selected Keyboard Composers and Keyboard Instruments is located in Appendix L.)

Although the piano was invented in the early part of the eighteenth century, it did not become widely used until the latter part of the century. In the nineteenth century, it went through numerous improvements that ultimately resulted in our present-day grand piano.

The upright piano was an innovation of the nineteenth century, and with this more economical and smaller instrument, pianos became a fixture in many American and European homes. In fact, it is said that in the 1850s there were more pianos than bathtubs in the United States, and in the early 1900s more pianos than telephones in the home.

---

*Willi Apel, *Harvard Dictionary of Music*, 2nd ed. (Cambridge, Mass.: Belknap Press of Harvard University Press, 1975), p. 669.

Grand piano (Steinway and Sons. Used by permission.)

Upright piano (Steinway and Sons. Used by permission.)

Electronic piano lab (Courtesy of Esau Products, Inc.)

Today pianos still come in the two eighteenth- and nineteenth-century shapes—the grand and the upright, also in recent years upright electronic pianos have been developed. Because the sound can be channeled through headphones, the electronic pianos are often used in a group piano setting.

For information on electronic keyboards (basic keyboards, digital pianos, and synthesizers), see the section Electronic Keyboards in Appendix J.

The Instrument

An acoustic piano produces its sound by strings being struck by hammers, which are put into action by the keys. The complex mechanism connecting this key-hammer motion is called the piano's *action.* The small but long pieces of felt-covered wood that lie above the strings are called the *dampers.* They move up and down with the action via connecting wires. The dampers allow the strings to vibrate freely the moment the hammer strikes and stop the vibration when the key is released.

A standard-size piano *keyboard* has eighty-eight keys: fifty-two white and thirty-six black keys. Some electronic pianos have shorter keyboards. The black keys alternate in groups of twos and threes up and down the keyboard. Pitches go higher as your fingers move to the right on the keyboard and lower as you move to the left.

Low   Middle   High

The modern piano has two or three foot-operated **pedals:** the **soft pedal** to the left, the **sostenuto pedal** in the middle, and the **damper pedal** to the right. Some upright pianos have only the soft and damper pedals. The damper pedal is used to connect and sustain tones, whereas the soft pedal, called **una corda** ("one string") **pedal,** is used to reduce the volume of sound. The sostenuto pedal (on a grand piano) permits the sustaining of a chord or a single note with the pedal while the hand is free to play other notes.

Elements of Music: Melody, Rhythm, Harmony, and Form

Although a pianist must develop skills in playing and reading music, he or she must also understand basic concepts about music. Music concepts may be studied within the framework of the elements of music. Most music of Western cultures contains four elements: melody, rhythm, harmony, and form. An individual element may be studied by itself; however, melody, rhythm, harmony, and form seldom occur singularly in music. Rather they are combined and interrelated to form musical compositions. Using the song "Norwegian Wood" as an example, one can explore how the elements of music are combined and interrelated to form a composition.

Norwegian Wood (This Bird Has Flown)

John Lennon (England, 1940–1980)
Paul McCartney (England, b. 1942)

And   when I   a - woke,   I   was a - lone,   this bird had   flown;

So   I   lit   a   fire,   Is - n't   it   good   Nor - we - gian   wood?

Melody

A **melody** *is a linear succession of sounds (pitches) and silences moving through time—that is, the horizontal structure of music.* Each melody is a unique combination of sounds and silences, which, when organized in a series, creates a sense of line or a meaningful musical shape.

Pitches in a melody may move up or down or remain the same. Listen to a performance of the melody of "Norwegian Wood." Notice how the melody moves up and down and often repeats. Connect the pitches on the score to discover the melodic **contour.**

Melodic contour

"Norwegian Wood" is distinctive not only for its pitches and resultant contour but also for its rhythm.

Rhythm

Rhythm *refers to all the durations of sounds and silences that occur in music as well as to the organization of these sounds and silences in time.* Perhaps the most fundamental ingredient of rhythm is the **beat** or pulse. When we listen to music, we often respond to the beat by tapping our feet "in time." The beat is that underlying pulsation that one feels recurring steadily as music moves through time. First, clap or tap the steady beat while "Norwegian Wood" is performed. Then, during a second performance, mark the beats under the music like this.

Beat:

Sounds and silences in a melody move through time with the beat or, more often, in longer or shorter durations than the beat. If you clap just the **rhythm of the melody** for "Norwegian Wood," these longer and shorter durations will be obvious.

Harmony

The simultaneous sounding of two or more tones not only gives melody support and color but also defines the melody itself. **Harmony** *is the vertical structure of music that moves through time and supports the melody.*

Chords are the principal building blocks of harmony. Chords include at least three pitches sounded simultaneously. On the piano, chords are generally played with the left hand (in the lower register), while melody is performed with the right hand (in the middle to upper register). (In popular music, chords are often indicated by an uppercase letter above the staff.) Locate the letter names of the chords in "Norwegian Wood," and listen to a performance with chords added to the melody.

Form

The overall design, plan, or order of a musical composition is known as its **form.** Musical ideas expressed with pitches and rhythms are organized by the composer in various ways to create artistic balance. Usually, smaller units of musical ideas are put together to create larger ones until finally an overall form or total piece of music emerges.

Music, as well as other art forms, utilizes unity and variety to achieve aesthetic balance. A brief musical idea called a **motive** is often used as the smallest unit to unify an entire composition. The recurring rhythmic motive in "Norwegian Wood" is:

If a motive may be likened to a few words in speech, a **phrase** corresponds to a clause or a simple sentence. As "Norwegian Wood" is performed, decide where the phrases begin and end; then mark the phrases with brackets. Notice which phrases are alike and which are different.

Just as motives are put together to build longer units called phrases, so phrases are combined to build still longer units known as **sections.** Some compositions have two or three sections, and others go beyond to create an extended sectional form.

Summary

To play the piano intelligently and sensitively, one must develop basic keyboard skills and understand basic concepts about melody, rhythm, harmony, and form. This preliminary discussion was simply an introduction to the elements of music. Each chapter in *PianoLab* focuses on various music concepts within these elements. The Timeline of Western Art Music and History (Appendix K) includes the specific characteristics of the elements of music from the Middle Ages to the present day.

❖ One

Position at the Keyboard

Sit directly in front of the middle of the keyboard, with feet flat on the floor. The manufacturer's label can be used as a reference on most pianos. Sit far enough back from the keyboard so that your arms can move freely and your body bends slightly forward at the waist. The piano bench should be high enough so your elbows are at keyboard level.

Playing Position

Drop your arms to your sides in a dangling position. Your arms should hang loosely from the shoulders. Keeping that same relaxed position, lift your hands to the keyboard. Rest your fingers on the keys. Notice that your hands are slightly arched, your fingers are gently curved, and your wrists are straight. The wrists should be level with the keys. Always try to retain that relaxed position with arched hands, curved fingers, and wrists straight but flexible. If you should begin to feel tense while playing, stop playing and drop your arms to your side in the dangling, relaxed position. Then begin again.

Hand Position

Your hands should stay as motionless as possible. Retain a natural rounded hand shape and keep your fingers as close to the keys as possible. Keys should be "struck," not pressed. As you strike (do not push) the keys, your hands should not move up and down with the fingers. Remember to play each key with the fleshy part of the finger. Fingernails must be short. As you play, your eyes should not be on the keys; rather, develop a "feel" for the keys—play by touch.

Correct position at the keyboard

Correct hand position

Names of the White Keys

The first seven letters of the alphabet are used to identify the white keys. This alphabetical pattern proceeds from left to right.

Keyboard Landmarks

Two keys, C and F, may be used as landmarks for identifying and learning the names of keys. C is located to the immediate left of the group of two black keys. **Middle C,** the C closest to the middle of the keyboard, is a focal point for beginning piano instruction. F is always located to the immediate left of the group of three black keys.

Keyboard Practice—White Keys

1. Start with the lowest white key and play up the keyboard, saying the names as you play. Change fingers so that you use them all. Reverse the naming by starting with the highest white key and playing downward, again saying the names of the keys as you play.

2. Locate and play every C on the keyboard; then play every D, E, F, G, A, and B.

3. Locate and play the following pitches as quickly as you can:

a high D	the lowest A	middle C
a low G	the highest F	the A above middle C
an E in the middle	a B in the middle	the G below middle C

Fingering

Good fingering is necessary for developing facility at the keyboard. The arabic numbers 1–5 are assigned to specific fingers of both hands. The thumbs are always 1; the index fingers, 2; the middle fingers, 3; the ring fingers, 4; and the little fingers, 5.

Finger numbers

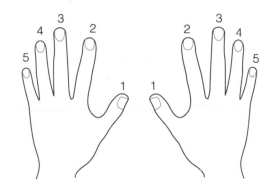

These numbers (usually written very small) appear above or below the notes in piano music to indicate the preferred fingering.

Finger numbers in music

Etude No. 7 (excerpt)   Louise Farrenc (France, 1804–1875)

Keyboard Practice—Finger Numbers

1. Practice saying the finger numbers aloud and moving the correct finger up and down.

2. As finger numbers are called out, play the correct fingers "in the air." Practice first with separate hands, then hands together.

3. At the keyboard, rest both hands on the pitches G, A, B, C, and D (LH = left hand; RH = right hand).

As someone plays and calls out finger numbers in rhythm, echo by playing correct fingers (and keys).

Examples:

Instructor: 5   5   5   5   Students: 5   5   5   5
               1   11   1   1   1   11   1   1
            33 3   3   3   33 3   3   3

4. Try to play a melody such as Beethoven's "Ode to Joy" (p. 64) dictated with finger numbers.

Playing the White Keys

1. With your left hand (LH), practice the following blues progression. Hold each key for four steady beats. When you are secure with the bass line, another player (or other players) can perform "Amanda's Blues" on p. 127 with you.

Blues progression

C C C C

F F C C

G F C C

2. Play the same progression with your right hand (RH) in the middle register of the piano. Check for correct fingering. Again, hold each key for four steady beats. While you play this higher part, another player (or other players) can perform "Walkin' Boogie," p. 249, or any boogie bass in Appendix H, 9–11.

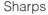

Other pieces that may be performed with this blues progression are on pp. 125, 126, 127, 140, 247, 248.

Sharps and Flats

The keys immediately to the left and right of the white keys are identified as **sharps** (♯) and **flats** (♭). Sharps indicate a move upward, or right, to the nearest black or white key. Flats signify a move downward, or left, to the nearest black or white key. Notice that E♯ and B♯ are white keys and F♭ and C♭ are white keys.

Sharps

Flats

Names of the Black Keys

The black keys use the same letter names as the white keys but with a sharp (♯) or a flat (♭) added. Each black key has two names. For example, the black key between C and D is called C♯ or D♭. C♯ and D♭ are referred to as **enharmonics,** that is, tones sounding the same pitch or key on the keyboard but identified by different letter names.

Keyboard Practice—Black Keys

1. Locate black keys by touch. Find black-key groupings; then play and name individual black keys.

2. Start with the lowest black key and play the black keys up the keyboard, saying the sharp names as you play. Repeat, saying the flat names for each key.

3. Locate and play the following pitches as quickly as you can.

   a high D♯   the highest E♭   the F♯ above middle C
   a low G♭   the lowest C♯   a high A♭
   an A♯ in the middle   a D♭ in the middle   the B♭ below middle C

Keyboard Practice—Sharps and Flats

1. Locate and play the black-key sharps; then play the white-key sharps.

2. Locate and play the black-key flats; then play the white key-flats.

3. Play the following accompaniment line with both hands. This part will fit with Leopold Mozart's "Minuet" (p. 220). Hold each pitch for three steady beats. ‖: :‖ are *repeat signs*, indicating that the pitches between the signs should be repeated.

"Minuet" accompaniment

Playing the Black Keys

The black keys are an excellent place to begin **improvisation,** or music performed extemporaneously. As you create different melodies and accompaniments, you will find that practically everything blends well together.

1. With your LH, play the following drone in a steady rhythm. (A **drone** may be two tones sounded together and repeated over and over.)

   Then try the ostinato with your RH. (An **ostinato** is a continuous repetition of a melodic or rhythmic pattern.)

Finally, perform the LH drone and the RH ostinato together. Repeat over and over in a steady rhythm. As soon as the two-hand part is coordinated, another player (or other players) can improvise melodies on the black keys with the drone-ostinato as an accompaniment.

Then try the drone in the RH and the ostinato in the LH:

2. By yourself, try playing the F♯–C♯ drone with your LH and improvising on any of the black keys with your RH. Keep the LH part steady. In the beginning, if you have trouble playing two different things, try matching the RH playing with the LH steady rhythm part. Then gradually experiment with your RH moving more freely on the black keys. Finally, try the drone with the RH and improvise with the LH.

3. Using only the black keys, play the following songs "by ear." The starting pitch for each is given.

   "Auld Lang Syne"—C♯
   "Merrily We Roll Along"—B♭
   "I'd Like to Teach the World to Sing"—E♭
   "Amazing Grace"—D♭
   "Tom Dooley"—C♯

Composing Project

Create a piano piece using the black keys. One part can be a drone or an ostinato, but it should establish the steady rhythmic background for the melody. The other hand should explore any of the black keys. Experiment with many ideas. If you wish to notate the pitches in your piece, write down the letter names of the notes. Lines can be used for shorter and longer durations. For example,

Ensemble Playing

Class piano situations offer opportunities for two or more students to play together—sometimes all on the same part with the teacher performing something different and sometimes with several pianists performing different parts. Performing with others requires playing exactly in time and careful listening for good balance in the ensemble.

Improvisation in the Boogie-Woogie Style

1. One pianist or group of pianists should set up the following **boogie-woogie** bass in the lower register. The pitches can be distributed between the two hands. "Walk" up and down the keys without stopping.

2. When the walking bass is secure, a second pianist or group of pianists should join in playing the same black keys but in the middle register and simultaneously in a slower rhythm. One idea would be to play the pitches at the beginning of each walking bass pattern.

3. When these two parts are secure, a third pianist can improvise on the same black keys but in the middle to upper register.
4. To end the improvisation, the third pianist(s) should drop out, then the second, and finally the first.

Repertoire

Indeterminacy

Indeterminacy refers to contemporary music in which the outcome or result is unpredictable. Contemporary composers give the performer(s) a framework within which to explore sounds, but no two performances using the framework are the same.

"Doodling" and "Sound Symbol Structure" are examples of indeterminate music. Look up information about the composers in Biographical Sketches of PianoLab Composers (Appendix M).

For "Doodling," follow the written directions of composer Tom Johnson. Before you begin, you could set up a tape recorder to record your piece. Later, play back and listen to your composition.

Doodling

Tom Johnson (United States, b. 1939)

Begin some very soft doodling with your right hand in the upper part of the keyboard. Continue the doodling as you read. Do not let your playing distract you from your reading, and do not let your reading distract you from your playing. The two must accompany each other. Now, without stopping the right-hand doodling, play a loud low note with your left hand, and sustain it for a moment. Continue the doodling and, whenever you feel the time is right, play another loud bass note. Do not wait too long between the loud low notes, but do not play them too close together either. Try not to worry about when you should or should not play another loud low note. If you become too involved with thinking about that, you will not be able to carry out your other tasks as well. Your attention should always be about equally divided between the three things: the reading, the right-hand doodling and the loud low notes.

Of course, you are quite limited in what you are permitted to play at the moment, and the music might become tedious after a while to someone who was only listening. But that is immaterial since these are *Private Pieces*, and are only for your own entertainment. The piece will not be tedious to you since it is not easy to do three things at once. The only way you can do all three well is by dividing your attention equally between them, so that you never ignore one of them. If you forget about the doodling, it will not sound the way you want it to sound. If you forget about the loud low notes, there will be a long awkward gap in the music. If you forget about the reading, you may miss some instruction or idea.

After another paragraph, you will be asked to play something else, but in the meantime continue playing and reading as you have been. If you find that you have been paying more attention to one of your tasks than to the other two, try to balance your attention more equally. Although no more instructions are necessary at the moment, the text is continuing in order to give you time to achieve a sense of balance between the three things, so that they seem to accompany one another. You have three more sentences in which to try to achieve this balance before going on to a new section of the piece. Now only two sentences, including this one, remain before the paragraph will end and you will be asked to do something else. This is the last sentence of this part of the piece.

Now stop playing, but continue reading. At some point during this paragraph, play a single note and sustain it. It may be loud or soft, high or low, black or white, but it must be a single note, and must be played only once. You may choose to play it early in the paragraph, or you may wish to play it toward the end of the paragraph. Perhaps you will want to read more of the text before making your decision. You must, however, remain within the limits of the paragraph. So if you have not played your note by this time, you must do so soon, as the paragraph is almost finished. You may wish to pause a moment before proceeding to the next paragraph, which will be quite demanding.

Resume the doodling with your right hand, as you did in the beginning of the piece, but this time let it gradually become more energetic. For a while it can be played by the right hand only, and should sound as it did at the beginning, but soon it should become faster. As it accelerates, you will probably want to use the left hand too, so that you can play more and more notes in less and less time. As the doodling becomes faster, you should also let it move into a wider range. By now the doodling should be noticeably more energetic than when you began this section. Do not let it increase too quickly, however, as there is still quite a ways to go before it reaches a peak. Gradually begin to use more and more of the keyboard and let the intensity increase until it is quite furious. Do not let the tension subside, even for a moment, and continue building until you are playing as wildly as you can. You may play anything necessary to maintain the high energy level. By now you should be playing as loud and fast as you can. You will perhaps find it more difficult to concentrate on the text now than when you were not playing so vigorously, but try to read the text as carefully as you have been, without making any sacrifices in your playing. Continue playing as wildly as you can, and look for ways that will enable you to play even more wildly. Do not be afraid to make booming or crashing sounds, if they will fit in with what you are already doing. When you find yourself running out of ideas or energy and want to end the piece, play one enormous crash and stop. Then listen for a moment to the silence.

Some composers use symbols instead of words or traditional notation to indicate their intentions. The following score illustrates a spatial way to symbolize a keyboard piece. Create a piece using Hays's symbol directions.

Sound Symbol Structure

Doris Hays (United States, b. 1941)

© 1982. Tallapoosa Music. Used by permission.

Symbol Chart

● = single tone

✳ = a **tone cluster** (play a cluster or group of adjacent tones simultaneously with fist or with palm of hand)

❃ = a tone cluster played louder

╲ = a hand **glissando** descending (a very rapid sliding passage down the white or black keys)

Performing Instructions

1. Decide on the amount of time (15–60 seconds) you want the structure to last. Then divide the score box into equal parts (three or four), giving each part an equal number of seconds. This will help you see at what point in time each symbol occurs. But remember that the duration of each symbol is indeterminate.

2. Explore two ways to play a tone cluster. The palm can produce a soft tone color by playing slowly, and the fist can produce a brilliant, percussive tone color by playing quickly.

3. For a LH glissando, start at the tips of your fingers and play keys to the edge of your palm. To play a glissando with your RH, start at the edge of your palm and play to your fingertips.

4. Experiment with the many different ways you can play this structure (right to left, left to right, upside down, and so on). Tape-record your structure, then play back the recorded structure. As the tape recorder plays, start several seconds later and perform your structure as an echo to the tape-recorded sounds.

5. After experimenting with the Hays structure, create and perform your own. Use any symbols that you like.

Technique Exercises

Technical development is an important part of piano playing. In addition to studying and playing the musical examples in each chapter, you also need to practice specific exercises to increase your technical facility and tonal control. In fact, each time you sit down to play the piano, make it a habit to warm up with a technical exercise or two.

The following technique exercises stress moving from one **octave** (eight notes) to another as smoothly and easily as possible. Try to develop a feel for the octave jumps. Find the notes by touch—do not look down.

Octave Jumps

An octave is the distance of eight notes between two pitches; the two pitches share the same letter name (C–C).

Octave

Exercise 1: Octave Jumps   Beginning with middle C, play C in three octaves with the RH thumb (1) going up the keyboard and the LH thumb (1) going down. Keep a steady beat, and allow one beat of silence between C's.

Example:

	C	"rest"	C	"rest"	C	"rest"
(Beats)	1	2	1	2	1	2

Exercise 2: Octave Jumps   Beginning with middle C, play C and D in three octaves with the RH fingers 1 and 2 going up the keyboard. Use the LH fingers 1 and 2 to play C and B going down. Keep a steady beat, and allow one beat of silence after the two notes.

Example (RH):

	C	D	"rest"	C	D	"rest"	C	D	"rest"
(Beats)	1	2	3	1	2	3	1	2	3

Exercise 3: Octave Jumps   Beginning with middle C, play C, D, and E in three octaves with the RH 1, 2, and 3 going up. Use the LH 1, 2, and 3 going down and C, B, and A. Again, leave a beat of silence between the three notes.

Example (LH):

	C	B	A	"rest"	C	B	A	"rest"	C	B	A	"rest"
(Beats)	1	2	3	4	1	2	3	4	1	2	3	4

Chapter Evaluation

1. Demonstrate the correct hand, arm, and body positions for piano playing.
2. Play and name any pitch on black or white keys.
3. Improvise a simple black-key melody. Either alternate the hands or play a drone with one hand and the melody with the other.
4. Demonstrate smooth and quick octave jumps with both hands with minimal looking at keys.
5. Identify the designated keys on the following chart. Write below the keyboard for the white keys and above the keyboard for the black keys.

6. A flat (♭) signifies a move _____ to the nearest key. A sharp (♯) signifies a move _____ to the nearest key.
7. ‖: :‖ are _____ signs indicating that the music between the signs should be _____ .
8. Write the enharmonic spelling for the given pitch.

C♯ __(D♭)__   B♭ _____   C _____   F♯ _____   F♭ _____

A♯ _____   E♭ _____   B _____   A♭ _____   G♯ _____

D♯ _____   G♭ _____   F _____   E♯ _____

D♭ _____   C♭ _____   E _____   B♯ _____

9. Performing music extemporaneously is known as _____.
10. Music in which the outcome or result is unpredictable is known as
_____ music.

TWO

Whole Steps and Half Steps

Major Five-Finger Pattern

Rhythm and Pitch Notation

Legato Touch

Parallel Motion

Independent Finger Action

Whole Steps and Half Steps

The distance from one pitch to another (*interval*) may be measured in whole steps and half steps. Pitches that are adjacent, or the shortest distance apart, are called **half steps** (for example, C to C♯, C♯ to D). There are two pairs of white keys that are naturally a half step apart—B to C and E to F.

half steps

All adjacent keys on the keyboard are a half step apart. (The **chromatic scale,** a twelve-tone scale, proceeds entirely in half steps.) One fingering approach for playing up or down in half steps is to use finger 3 on black keys and fingers 1 and 2 on white keys (2 only on consecutive white keys). Notice that the LH fingering going down is the same as the RH going up and vice versa. Begin on any key and play up every black and white key.

A **whole step** includes two half steps; for example, the interval from C to D is a whole step because it is made up of two half steps (C to C♯ and C♯ to D). Therefore, on the keyboard, one key (black or white) always comes between the pitches of a whole step. Begin on any key and play up in whole steps. Say the letter names, using sharps to identify black keys. Then find a new pitch and play down in whole steps. Say the letter names, using flats to name the black keys.

whole steps

Major Five-Finger Pattern

The whole-half step arrangement of the *major five-finger pattern* (the first five notes of a major scale) is as follows:

All five notes in the pattern are identified by different letter names. The first pitch of the pattern is called the *tonic* or *do.* Any key or pitch can be used as the tonic.

Playing the C Major Five-Finger Pattern

Tonic

LH 5 4 3 2 1   RH 1 2 3 4 5

1. Play each key of the C major five-finger pattern first up and then down. Say or sing the pitch names as you play.
2. Say the whole-half step arrangement as you play the C major five-finger pattern: tonic, whole step, whole step, half step, whole step.

3. Play the C major five-finger pattern, calling out the correct finger numbers. Notice that with the RH, the tonic (bottom note or starting note) is played with the thumb (1), whereas with the LH, the tonic (bottom note or starting note) is played with the little finger (5).

4. Try Technique Exercise 1 (at end of this chapter) with the C major five-finger pattern.

5. Play the familiar song "When the Saints Go Marching In" with the C major five-finger pattern. Follow these steps:

   a. Clap the rhythm of the melody.

   b. Sing the finger numbers of the melody (RH) while playing the song "in the air."

   c. Locate the C major five-finger pattern on the keyboard.

   d. Play the melody (RH) while singing the finger numbers. Keep your eyes on the numbers in the book.

   e. Play the melody while singing letter names aloud. Again, keep your eyes on the book.

   f. Practice the LH part. Hold each note for four steady beats. Play the accompaniment "in the air" while singing the finger numbers.

   g. Locate the LH position at the keyboard. Play the accompaniment while singing the melody.

   h. Two players or groups of players can perform the melody and accompaniment, or one player can play both. (A Piano 2 part for the teacher follows.)

When the Saints Go Marching In

Piano 1 (Students)   Black American Spiritual

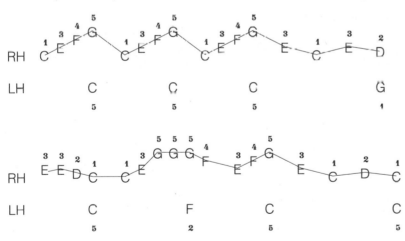

Piano 2 (Teacher)

arr. Eric Tamm

Introduction

Oh, when the saints

cresc.

Playing Major Five-Finger Patterns

1. Spell and play the major five-finger patterns on the given tonic. Use a different letter name for each note. Remember to locate the tonic with the RH thumb and the LH little finger. Rest the other fingers on the four remaining pitches in the major pattern.

a. C ___ ___ ___ ___

b. D ___ ___ ___ ___

c. E ___ ___ ___ ___

d. F ___ ___ ___ ___

e. G ___ ___ ___ ___

f. A ___ ___ ___ ___

g. B ___ ___ ___ ___

h. C♯ ___ ___ ___ ___

i. E♭ ___ ___ ___ ___

j. F♯ ___ ___ ___ ___

k. A♭ ___ ___ ___ ___

l. B♭ ___ ___ ___ ___

2. Practice Technique Exercise 1 at the end of this chapter in different major five-finger patterns.

❖ RHYTHM

Notes and Rests

Rhythm refers to all the **durations** of sounds and silences in music. **Notes** are the symbols used to represent durational sounds, and **rests** are used to indicate silences.

Note parts

A notehead can be open (longer-duration notes) or solid (shorter-duration notes). The stems extend upward from the right or downward from the left of the notehead. Flags on both upward and downward stems always curl to the right.

Notes		Rests	
o	whole note	▬	whole rest
♩ ♩	half note	▬	half rest
♩ ♩	quarter note	𝄽	quarter rest
♪ ♪	eighth note	𝄾	eighth rest
♪ ♪	sixteenth note	𝄿	sixteenth rest

Beams

Notes with flags are frequently beamed together in groups.

Relative Note Durations

Notes are of relative duration, one to the other.

1 whole note
equals

2 half notes
equal

4 quarter notes
equal

8 eighth notes
equal

16 sixteenth notes

Beat and Meter

Most music has a steady **beat** or pulse. Beats are organized into groups, referred to as **meter.** Some beats are stressed more than others and become grouped in twos (**duple meter**), threes (**triple meter**), or fours (**quadruple meter**). The first beat in each meter is a strong beat or primary **accent** (´) and is followed by weaker, unaccented beats (˘). In quadruple meter, there is a secondary accent (−) on beat three.

Meter

Duple Meter (2s):   ´ ˘
                      1 2

Triple Meter (3s):   ´ ˘ ˘
                      1 2 3

Quadruple Meter (4s): ´ ˘ − ˘
                      1 2 3 4

Meter Signatures

The two numbers, one above the other, that appear at the very beginning of a piece of music constitute the **meter signature** or **time signature.** The top number specifies the beat grouping, or meter, and the bottom number indicates the note that gets the beat.

2 → 2 beats per measure
4 → ♩ receives 1 beat

3 → 3 beats per measure
4 → ♩ receives 1 beat

4 → 4 beats per measure
4 → ♩ receives 1 beat

Frequently Used Meter Signatures in Simple Meter

The following meters are referred to as **simple** because the beat in each divides into two equal parts.

Duple Meter: $\frac{2}{4}$ $\frac{2}{2}$ or ¢ (alla breve)

Triple Meter: $\frac{3}{8}$ $\frac{3}{4}$ $\frac{3}{2}$

Quadruple Meter: $\frac{4}{8}$ $\frac{4}{2}$ $\frac{4}{4}$ or C (common time)

Bar Lines

Vertical **bar lines** are used to indicate the meter or beat grouping and divide the music into **measures**. A double bar line is used at the end of a composition or section.

Rhythm Exercise 1: Duple and Quadruple Meters (○, ♩, ♩, ♫) Clap, chant, or play the following rhythmic lines on any key(s). The numbers under the notes refer to each consecutive beat in the measure (the top number of the meter signature), and these numbers are often spoken to aid in reading rhythms. (The numbers in parentheses are not clapped or played, but are counted.) Use the number counting system or any counting method recommended by your instructor.

Performing Melodies

1. Determine the number of beats each note receives in "Love Somebody." Count the beats as you clap the rhythm. Play the melody using the C major five-finger pattern, hands separately and hands together.

Love Somebody

American Folk Song

2. Determine the number of beats each note receives in "Chorale Melody." Clap and count the rhythm of the melody before playing it with the G major five-finger pattern.

Chorale Melody*

---

*A **chorale** is a hymn tune of the German Protestant church. Many compositions (especially in the seventeenth and eighteenth centuries) have been based on chorale melodies.

Rhythm Exercise 2: Two-Part Rhythms   When playing the piano, one must perform two rhythms simultaneously—one with the RH and one with the LH. These examples should be performed by tapping or playing on any key the notes on the bottom line with one hand and the notes on the top line with the other hand. Perform each line separately, then hands together.

❖ **MELODY**

Treble and Bass Clef Notation

Pitches are notated on a *staff* (five lines and four spaces). Two staves, often called the **grand** or **great staff,** are used in piano music. The upper staff specifies the higher notes, usually played by the RH, and the lower staff identifies the lower notes, usually played by the LH. A **treble clef,** or G clef, encircles the second line (G) of the higher staff. A **bass clef,** or F clef, is written with a dot above and below the fourth line (F) and is placed on the lower staff. Short lines, called **leger** (or **ledger**) **lines,** can be added above and below the staff to extend the pitch range. Note that stems go up on notes below the middle line of the staff and go down on notes on and above the middle line.

The following grand staff includes the notation for white keys of the piano. When black keys are indicated, sharps and flats are placed *before* the note on the same line or space as the notehead or *after* the clef sign as a key signature on each staff of music. (See Appendix B for a grand staff with notation for both white and black keys.)

Grand staff

Pitch-Reading Exercise

1. Beginning with the lowest C on the bass clef staff above, play and name aloud the bass clef notes up to middle C (with your left hand), and then play the notes going back down.

2. Beginning with middle C on the treble clef staff, play and name the treble clef notes up to high C (with your right hand), and then reverse the naming and playing back to middle C. Memorize the names and their staff positions.

3. Sing the letter names and play the following musical examples in different major five-finger patterns. Look at the music, not at your hands, to develop confidence in your sense of touch.

C major

G major

D major

A major

F major

4. Notate "Love Somebody" and "Chorale Melody" (p. 29) in treble and bass clef notation. Then play while reading from staff notation.

Key Signatures

The sharps (♯) or flats (♭) to be played throughout a piece are traditionally placed *after* the clef sign on each staff and *before* the meter signature. This grouping of sharps or flats is called a **key signature**. For example, if there is a sharp on the F line, all F's in the music should be performed as F-sharp rather than F-natural (♮). If a flat appears on the B line, all B's should be performed as B-flat rather than B-natural.

Key signature

  Play all F's as F-sharp

Key signature

  Play all B's as B-flat

Sometimes sharps or flats may appear in the key signature and not be used in the composition. In addition to specifying which notes will be sharped or flatted, the key signature identifies the **key** of the piece. Chapters 6 and 9 present information on major and minor key signatures.

GB

Performing Melodies

In the following melodies, your two hands move in the same direction (**parallel motion**) and play the same notes an octave apart. Practice Exercise 2: Parallel Motion later in this chapter.

Then, determine the major five-finger pattern for each of the following melodies. Find the last note (usually the tonic), and check for sharps and flats in the key signature. Practice hands separately and hands together.

Folk Melody 1

Russian Folk Melody

Folk Melody 2

Folk Melody 3

Composing Project

Create a black-key melody using the following rhythm. Notate the letter names of the pitches above the rhythm or on a staff. Use either all sharps or all flats; do not mix the two. Try a drone with your melody.

Ensemble Playing

Before playing Recreation I and II, determine the meaning of *andante, andante cantabile,* and *8va sempre,* by referring to Appendix A.

Recreation I*

Piano 1 (Students)

Andante

Arnoldo Sartorio (Germany, 1853–?)

---

*To perform Piano 1 with two students at a piano, one student plays the part as written while the second student plays the part two octaves lower.

Piano 2 (Teacher)

Andante

Recreation II

Piano 1 (Students)

Andante cantabile

Arnoldo Sartorio (Germany, 1853–?)

Piano 2 (Teacher)

Andante cantabile

(8va bassa sempre)

(8va bassa sempre)

(8va bassa sempre)

Repertoire

Visually analyze each of the following pieces, and determine the tonic, the major five-finger pattern, and the meter for each. Look up information about the composers in the *PianoLab* Composers section (Appendix M). (No information about Beyer has been located.) After learning each composer's birthdate and death date, determine the historical period (for example, Classic) in which each composer lived by referring to the Timeline of Western Art Music and History (Appendix K). Review the musical characteristics of the period. Look up **tempo** (moderato) and **dynamic** (*f mf*) terms in Appendix A.

"Unison Melody" and "Melody" should be performed *legato* (playing in a smooth, connected manner), often indicated by a curved line (**slur**) above or below the pitches. Review Technique Exercise 1 in this chapter. Then practice each piece hands separately and hands together. Notice that the two hands move in the same direction (parallel motion) for "Unison Melody" and "Melody."

Unison Melody (No. 1 from *First Term at the Piano*)

Moderato

Béla Bartók (Hungary, 1881–1945)

Melody

Moderato

Ferdinand Beyer (1803–1863)

Technique Exercises

Before practicing any of these technique exercises, check your hand position at the keyboard.

Are your hands slightly arched?

Are your fingers gently curved? Is the fleshy part of your fingers striking the keys?

Are your fingernails short?

Are your wrists and arms straight but flexible?

Exercise 1: *Legato Touch*   Legato touch requires playing in a smooth, connected manner. You must hold each key, lifting as you play the next key without blurring pitches together. To do this, you need to maintain a good hand position and a flexible wrist. Allow only one key to sound at a time. Let the weight of your arms shift from one finger to the next while you keep a good hand position and a flexible wrist.

The following examples can be played with any major five-finger pattern, hands separately and hands together.

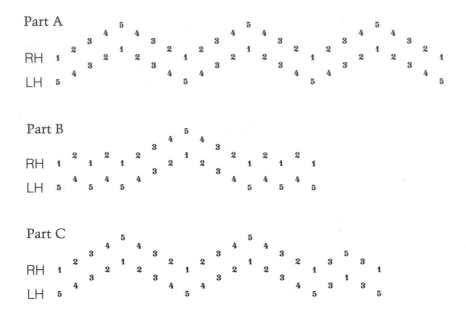

Part A

Part B

Part C

Exercise 2: *Parallel Motion*   Practice the following parallel motion example hands together and with each hand separately. Strive for evenness of tones, and connect pitches as smoothly as possible. Play in the C, G, D, A, and F major patterns.

Exercise 3: *Independent Finger Action*   Your fingers must become independent and strong. Practice this exercise very slowly. Begin with a good hand position. Make certain that the fingers strike the keys from a height of about half an inch without moving the top of the hand and wrist. Play legato (hold each key, lifting as you play the next key). Play the following patterns, beginning on any note.

Part A

Part B

Chapter Evaluation

1. Demonstrate whole- and half-step distances at the keyboard.

2. Play a major five-finger pattern on the following tonics: C, G, D, A, and F.

3. Clap, chant, or play the rhythm of any melody or rhythm example in this chapter.

4. Demonstrate keyboard recognition of pitches notated in the treble and bass clefs.

5. Perform one of the melodies in this chapter with pitch and rhythmic accuracy and using correct fingering.

6. Demonstrate legato playing by performing an example from Technique Exercise 1 in this chapter.

7. Identify each interval as a half step or a whole step.

(H)

8. Identify the whole-half step arrangement of the major five-finger pattern:

1 ___(whole)__ 2 _____ 3 _____ 4 _____ 5

9. Identify the letter names for all the treble and bass clef pitches in the following example.

Sonata XXXIV, (K. 309) (excerpt)   Domenico Scarlatti (Italy, 1685–1757)

10. Notate the following major five-finger patterns on the staff and keyboard chart. Circle the tonic pitch for each. When **accidentals** are needed, write the sharps or the flats on the staff *before* the pitches on the *same* line or in the *same* space.

11. Write numbers under the notes to refer to each consecutive beat in the measure.

1 & 2 & 3 & 4 &

12. Duple meter refers to beat groupings in _____ .
Triple meter refers to beat groupings in _____ .
Quadruple meter refers to beat groupings in _____ .

13. Create and notate four measures of rhythm for each of the following meter signatures.

Three

Interval Reading

Learning to recognize musical distances—**intervals**—is important in reading and performing music. You need to first identify intervals in music notation and then develop a feel for the keyboard distances of those intervals. For example, when notes are on adjacent lines and spaces, you move from one piano key to the next (and from one letter name to the next). This interval is called a *second*. C to D is a second.

When notes skip from one space to the next space or from one line to the next line, you skip one piano key (and one letter name). This interval is called a *third*. C to E is a third.

The following intervals are commonly used in major five-finger melodies. All intervals can appear with the two pitches occurring successively (called a *melodic interval*) or with the two pitches sounding simultaneously (called a *harmonic interval*).

Intervals in the Major Five-Finger Pattern

Intervals are identified by *number* and *quality*. The number identification is determined by the letter names of the two notes.

C major

The quality of each interval is determined by the precise number of half steps between the two notes. In the major five-finger pattern, the qualities of the intervals formed with the tonic pitch are either major or perfect.

C major

Interval Exercises

1. Read and play each interval in the major five-finger pattern. Feel the distances and listen to the sound of each interval.
2. Play these intervals in the following pattern. Stress independent finger action, and work for a legato sound.

Major Five-Finger Interval Exercise

C major

Performing Melodies—Interval Reading

As you perform the following melodies, first *look* at the notation and try to identify the interval distances between pitches by sight. Then try to *feel* the keyboard distances of those intervals as you play each piece. For additional interval reading, perform any of the pieces in Chapter 2 noticing interval distances.

Melody　　　　　　　　　　　　　　　　　　　Louis Köhler (Germany, 1820–1886)

French Folk Melody 1

Folk Melody 4

Transposition

Changing a melody from one key (scale) or major pattern to another is called
transposition. For example, "The Old Oak Tree" is notated in the G major five-
finger pattern. If this melody is changed to the F major pattern, it is referred to as
being transposed.

The Old Oak Tree

G major   English Round

F major

There are several ways to transpose. One way is to identify each pitch in the
original by number and then change each number to the letter name of the new
pattern.

Original:	G	A	B	C	D
	1	2	3	4	5
	do	re	mi	fa	sol
Transposed:	F	G	A	B♭	C
	1	2	3	4	5
	do	re	mi	fa	sol

Another way is to calculate the interval distances (up or down) between the original version and the new one. For example, "The Old Oak Tree" is in the G major pattern and the transposed version is in the F major pattern, *a whole step down*. Therefore, each pitch in the original would be transposed down a whole step.

Transposition Practice

1. Perform the two versions of "The Old Oak Tree" just given. Feel the similarity in keyboard distances for both.

2. At the keyboard, transpose some or all of the following pieces (or any in Chapter 2 or 3).

   "Folk Melody 1," p. 34, to G major
   "Russian Folk Melody," p. 34, to C major
   "Unison Melody," p. 39, to D major
   "Melody" by Beyer, p. 39, to G major
   "Melody" by Köhler, p. 46, to D major
   "French Folk Melody 1," p. 46, to G major
   "Folk Melody 4," p. 47, to C major

3. Notate any or all of the preceding transposed pieces.

❖ RHYTHM

Rhythm Exercise 1: Duple and Quadruple Meters (o, 𝅝, 𝅘𝅥, 𝅘𝅥𝅮, 𝄽, 𝄼) Clap, chant, or play the following rhythmic lines on any key(s). Use the number counting system or any counting method recommended by your instructor.

6.

7.

8.

9.

1 & 2 & 1 & 2 & 1 & 2 & 1 & (2 &)

10.

1 & 2 & 1 & 2 & 1 & 2 & 1 & (2 &)

Rhythm Exercise 2: Two-Part Rhythms   Perform by tapping or playing on any key(s) the notes on the bottom line with one hand and the notes on the top line with the other hand. Perform each line hands separately and then hands together.

1.

2.

3.

4.

5.

6.

❖ HARMONY

Chords

The building blocks of harmony are **chords.** *A chord consists of three or more pitches a third apart, sounded simultaneously.* Chords are often played with the left hand to provide an accompaniment for a melody.

Since playing three or more notes simultaneously may be a challenge to beginning pianists, chord accompaniments can be simplified by playing only one tone of the chord. Of the chord tones, the **chord root** (bottom note) is the strongest.

Chord Symbols

In jazz and in popular and folk music, the names of chord roots are used in a symbol system called *lead sheet notation.* Uppercase letters are written above the staff, specifying what chords should be used and when they should be played. The single pitch indicated by the chord symbol is the chord root. (When a number appears next to a capital letter, a four-note chord is indicated.)

To add a chord-root accompaniment to a melody, play with your left hand the single pitch indicated by the chord symbol. Play the roots an octave lower than the melody and on the strong beats of the measure. Play the same chord root until a new symbol is given.

Me and Bobby McGee (excerpt)

Kris Kristofferson (United States, b. 1936)
Fred Foster

Melody

Bust - ed   flat   in   Ba - ton Rouge,   Head - in'   for   the   trains;

Chord root played

Performing Melodies with Chord-Root Accompaniment

1. Locate the two chord symbols for each melody. Notice that the chord roots for each are the first (I) and fifth (V) tones of the major five-finger pattern. When playing the chord roots in the LH, use the little finger for the first, or tonic, and the thumb for the fifth. When playing the chord roots in the RH, use the thumb for the tonic and the little finger for the fifth. Play a chord root in each measure.

Example:

Chord Symbols:	C				G7
Chord Roots:	C				G
C Major Pattern:	C	D	E	F	G
Number Position:	I				V7

Little River

German Folk Melody

C (I)   G7 (V7)   C

Jim-Along Josie

American Folk Melody

G   D7   G   D7   G

English Folk Melody 1

Chilean Folk Melody

2. At the keyboard, transpose one or two of the preceding folk melodies ("Little River," "Jim-Along Josie," English, and Chilean) to other major patterns. To transpose the chord-root accompaniment, remember the chord roots will be the first and fifth pitches of the new major pattern.

Performing Chord Roots from Staff Notation

1. Chord roots for the following melodies are written out in the bass and treble clefs. Strive for a good balance between hands.

Hungarian Folk Melody 1

Transpose to G major

Danish Folk Melody

Transpose to F major

American Folk Melody 1

Transpose to G major

2. Write out the chord-root accompaniment in staff notation for "Little River," p. 51; "Jim-Along Josie," p. 51; "English Folk Melody 1," p. 52; and "Chilean Folk Melody," p. 52.

Composing Project

Create an eight-measure melody based on a selected major five-finger pattern. Be sure to end your melody on the tonic. Use the following rhythm, and notate the melody in staff notation.

Ensemble Playing*

Love Somebody

Piano 1

American Folk Song

Piano 2

*These ensemble pieces marked for two pianos may also be performed on one piano by playing the Piano 1 part an octave higher and the Piano 2 part an octave lower.

J'ai du bon Tabac

Piano 1

French Folk Song

Piano 2

Repertoire

Visually analyze each of the following pieces, determining the tonic, the major five-finger pattern, and the meter for each. Look up information about the composers in the Biographical Sketches of *PianoLab* Composers (Appendix M). Then determine the historical period for each by reviewing the Timeline of Western Art Music and History (Appendix K).

In "Op. 117, No. 5," both the RH and the LH parts are notated in the treble clef. Check the meaning of *op.* **(opus)** in the Glossary and *allegretto* and *allegro* in Appendix A.

Op. 117, No. 5

Allegretto

Cornelius Gurlitt (Germany, 1820–1901)

In "Allegro" the RH stays within the C major five-finger pattern (an octave above middle C). The LH, however, covers the range of an octave. Practice the LH fingering and range before playing the piece with hands together.

Allegro

Daniel Gottlob Türk (Germany, 1750–1813)

Technique Exercises

Before playing any of these exercises, check your hand position. Make sure you are comfortably seated at the piano.

Exercise 1: Contrary Motion Pianists must learn to coordinate their two hands playing together. When two hands move in opposite directions, the motion is called **contrary.**

Practice the following contrary motion exercise, keeping the wrists flexible and the arms moving in a gentle outward and upward movement for each two-measure pattern in Part A. In Part B, the movements will be reversed. Transpose this exercise to the major five-finger patterns of G, D, A, E, F, and B.

Part A

Part B

Exercise 2: Independent Hands and Hand Coordination   This exercise should be practiced in two parts. The first (Part A) focuses on the RH moving in quarter notes while the LH moves in whole notes. Part B reverses this rhythmic movement. Transpose to other major patterns.

Part A

Part B

Exercise 3: Register Change   Practice hands together in contrary motion. Try to move as smoothly as possible from one octave to another. Work for agility in the register changes. Transpose to other major patterns.

Chapter Evaluation

1. Demonstrate intervals of perfect unisons, major seconds, major thirds, perfect fourths, and perfect fifths at the keyboard.

2. At the keyboard, transpose "Folk Melody 2" on p. 34 from the F major five-finger pattern to the G major pattern.

3. Perform a chord-root accompaniment for "Chilean Folk Melody," p. 52.

4. Demonstrate hand coordination in *contrary motion* by performing Technique Exercise 1 in this chapter.

5. Label the following intervals by quality and number, such as P5. Using the keyboard chart, count the number of half steps between the two notes. Remember: P1 = 0, M2 = 2, M3 = 4, P4 = 5, P5 = 7.

6. Complete the specified intervals by notating the second pitch above (↑) or below (↓) the given pitch (as in melodic intervals). Use the keyboard chart above to count the needed half steps for each.

7. Transpose Op. 117, No. 5, on p. 54, to the D major five-finger pattern. Notate the transposition. When accidentals are needed, write the sharps or
the flats on the staff *before* the notes on the *same* line or in the *same* space.

8. Notate the chord roots (in the bass clef) for each chord in the excerpt from
"Leavin' on a Jet Plane."

Leavin' on a Jet Plane (excerpt)   John Denver (United States, b. 1943)

Four

❖ RHYTHM

Anacrusis

The notes in the incomplete measure found at the beginning of many pieces are called the **anacrusis,** the **upbeat** or "pickup" notes. Often in short melodies, the anacrusis and an incomplete last measure combine to make one complete measure. The notes in the anacrusis are unaccented and actually anticipate the accent of the first beat in the first full measure.

Allegro (excerpt from Sonata in E Minor)   Marianne Martines (Austria, 1744–1812)

Beginning of section   *Ending of section*

Rhythm Exercise 1: Anacrusis, Triple Meter   Clap, chant, or play the following rhythmic lines on any key(s). To perform the rhythmic lines that include an upbeat, or anacrusis, count a full measure of beats first; then count the beat that precedes the upbeat. Be sure you know on which beat the upbeat falls.

Rhythm Exercise 2: Coordinated Rhythms (2 hands) Analyze, then perform these examples by tapping or playing on any key the notes on the bottom line with your LH and the notes on the top line with your RH. Perform each line separately and then perform the lines together.

Performing Melodies with Anacrusis

For the following three pieces, determine on which beat the anacrusis falls. Count a full measure of beats first; then count the beat or beats that precede the anacrusis.

Minuet 10 (excerpt)　　　　　　　　　　　Franz Joseph Haydn (Austria, 1732–1809)

Transpose to G major

German Folk Melody 1

Transpose to G major

German Folk Melody 2

Transpose to C major

Dotted Notes and Rests

A dot prolongs the duration of a note or a rest. One dot placed to the right of a notehead or a rest increases the duration by one half the note's value.* For example, a dotted half note (♩.) is equal to the total duration of three quarter notes: ♩. = ♩♩♩ (A dotted note or rest divides naturally into three equal parts.)

Dotted Notes

𝅝·	dotted whole note
♩. 𝅗𝅥·	dotted half note
♩. ♩·	dotted quarter note
♪. ♪·	dotted eighth note
♬. ♬·	dotted sixteenth note

Dotted Rests

▬·▬	dotted whole rest
▬·	dotted half rest
𝄽·	dotted quarter rest
𝄾·	dotted eighth rest
𝄿·	dotted sixteenth rest

___
*A dot *over* or *under* a notehead means that the note should be played in a detached, disconnected manner called *staccato* (♩·).

Rhythm Exercise 3: Dotted Notes   Clap, chant, or play the following rhythmic lines on any key(s). Determine the number of counts each dotted note receives.

Performing Melodies with Dotted Notes

Visually analyze each melody; then count and clap the rhythm of each. Determine the number of beats each dotted note receives, and mark the beats for each measure.

English Folk Melody 2

Transpose to D major

Ode to Joy (from the Fourth Movement,
Symphony No. 9, Op. 125)

Ludwig van Beethoven (Germany, 1770–1827)

Transpose to E major

Mexican Wedding Song
Arranged by Ritchie Valens (United States, 1941–1959)

La Bamba (excerpt)

❖ **HARMONY**

Triads

The most common chords are built by arranging intervals of thirds one above the other. The most basic chord of tonal music is the **triad,** a chord with three pitches. The three pitches of any triad are identified by the terms *root, third,* and *fifth.* The root also gives the triad its letter name: C, F, and so on.

Major Triad

By combining the *first, third,* and *fifth* pitches of the major five-finger pattern, one forms a **major triad.** The major triad always includes a *major third* (four half steps) between the root and the third, a *minor third* (three half steps) between the third and the fifth, and a *perfect fifth* (seven half steps) between the root and the fifth.

Performing Major Triads in Block-Chord Form

Practice the major triad in *block-chord form* (chord tones played simultaneously) in the following positions at the keyboard. Sit centered at the keyboard and far enough back to allow freedom of movement. To play the chords, push keys down simultaneously, with equal weight on each key. Try to connect playings of the chord as smoothly as possible. Be careful not to overlap the chords when hands cross. Transpose to G, F, D, A, and E.

Block Chord Exercise: Major Triad

Part A

Part B

Performing Major Triads in Arpeggio Form

These exercises use the major triad in *broken-chord*, or **arpeggio**, *form* (chord tones played one after the other). Again, connect chord tones as smoothly as you can and use the hand-over-hand technique when specified. Hold the chord shape in the hand and touch each new key's location just before playing. Transpose to the major triads of F, G; D, A, E; and D♭, A♭, E♭. Learn the feel of these chords grouped by color of keys.

Arpeggio Exercise: Major Triad

Part A

Part B

Tonic Chord

The first pitch of the major five-finger pattern is called the **tonic,** and the chord built on the first step is called the *tonic chord* or I chord. The tonic chord for the major pattern is a major triad.

C major five-finger pattern—Tonic chord

Tonic Chord and Major Five-Finger Pattern

Locate the major triad build on the tonic for each major five-finger pattern. Play the following example in these major five-finger patterns: C, G, F; D, A, E; and D♭, A♭, E♭.

C major

Performing Melodies with Tonic Chord Accompaniments

The first three melodies are accompanied with the tonic chord of the major pattern. Perform with a good balance of sound between the melody and the chord (melody should dominate).

Whistle Daughter   American Folk Song

Transpose to D major

Dressed in Blue   American Folk Song

Transpose to G major

Umptum Lady   American Folk Song

Transpose to A major

The next three melodies have the tonic chord as part of their accompaniment. Observe the dynamic markings of *forte* (loud) and *piano* (soft).

Little River

German Folk Melody

Transpose to D major

American Folk Melody 2

Transpose to F major

Folk Melody 5

Transpose to E major

❖ **FORM**

Phrases

The overall design, plan, or order of a musical composition is referred to as its *form*. Most of the melodies studied so far are of a simple folk-song design. Even though the melodies are only eight to twelve measures long, they divide into smaller musical ideas known as **phrases.** In many of these melodies, the phrases (musical clauses or sentences) span approximately four measures. Pianists often punctuate the end of a phrase by a momentary lift or "breath."

Parallel Phrases

When two phrases begin with the same pitches and include almost identical material, the paired phrases are said to be *parallel*.

"Israeli Folk Melody 1" illustrates parallel phrases (phrase 2 is almost identical to phrase 1). As you perform this melody with chord roots, be sure to lift slightly at the end of the phrases. Notice that once you have learned the first phrase, you have almost learned the entire melody.

Israeli Folk Melody 1

Contrasting Phrases

When a second phrase (especially its beginning) includes musical materials that are different from those of the first phrase, the phrases are *contrasting*. Often one feels a question-and-answer type dialogue in paired contrasting phrases.

"Folk Melody 6" is an example of contrasting phrases. Perform this melody with chord roots, marking the ends of phrases with a slight lift.

Folk Melody 6

Identify parallel or contrasting phrases in the following pieces:

"German Folk Melody 2" (p. 62) _____

"Minuet 10" (excerpt) by Haydn (p. 61) _____

"Russian Folk Melody" (p. 34) _____

"Ode to Joy" by Beethoven (p. 64) _____

"Allegro" by Türk (p. 55) _____

Composing Project

Compose two melodies illustrating parallel and contrasting phrase structure. The first phrase for each melody is provided. Write a phrase of the same length that is parallel or contrasting. Use the F major pattern, and make sure you conclude on the tonic. Play your melodies.

Melody 1—Parallel phrases

↑ tonic

Melody 2—Contrasting phrases

↑ tonic

Ensemble Playing

Duet Exercise 32*

Piano 1 (Students)

Andante   Ferdinand Beyer (1803–1863)

Piano 2 (Teacher)

Andante

---

*To perform with two students at one piano, one student plays Piano 1 as written while another plays Piano 1 two octaves lower.

It's Natural to Have a Flat

Piano 1 (Students)

Easy swing   Lee Evans (United States, b. 1933)

The **natural sign** (♮) cancels a flat or a sharp.

Piano 2 (Teacher)

Easy swing

Repertoire

Visually analyze the two repertoire pieces, and determine the tonic, the finger position, the meter, and the phrase structure for each. Locate information about the two composers in the Biographical Sketches of *PianoLab* Composers (Appendix M). Refer to the Timeline of Western Art Music and History (Appendix K) to place the composers in a historical period. Check the meaning of dynamic marking **mf** in Appendix A. Memorize one of the pieces.

Memorizing

Memorizing music requires several different kinds of skills. It is not enough to keep repeating a piece until your fingers can play it automatically. Your mind needs to guide your fingers for a lasting memorization.

First, a thorough understanding of the melody, rhythm, harmony, and form is necessary for recalling the total "picture" of the piece under study. This is achieved through analysis. Second, after you have performed a piece many times and studied the technical aspects, your fingers should know the physical movements. Third, you must be able to remember aurally the pitches and their rhythmic values.

Guidelines for Memorizing Pieces

1. You are ready to memorize when you can play a piece with pitch and rhythmic accuracy and correct fingering (hands separately and hands together). In addition, you should have a sound knowledge of the characteristics of melody, rhythm, and form.

2. When step 1 is accomplished, you really only need to work on aurally recalling the pitches and rhythm. Begin by dividing the piece into smaller parts. (In short compositions, these parts would be phrases.) Learn to play these smaller parts from memory with each hand separately. When you can do this easily, try playing each hand alone but using just one finger (index). This is a good test to see if you know the notes aurally without the aid of physical involvement.

3. Play the smaller parts hands together from memory. Try playing with your eyes closed.

4. Combine the smaller parts until the whole piece is memorized. Then try playing the piece with your eyes closed.

The Kabalevsky piece has both the LH and the RH parts notated in the treble clef. (The LH part extends beyond the five-finger pattern.) The short horizontal line above or below a note ($\bar{p}$) indicates that the note should be performed with a slight stress and that the tone should be sustained. Observe the phrasing, and work for a legato touch.

Melody, Op. 39, No. 1 (from *24 Little Pieces*)

Moderato   Dmitri Kabalevsky (Russia, 1904–1987)

In "3 White-Note Clusters," a twentieth-century composition, the white and black rectangles are tone clusters of three notes. (Clusters are bunched seconds played simultaneously. Pitches in the cluster are determined by the position on the staff.) Play the *blocked clusters* with fingers 2, 3, and 4 in each hand.

Blocked clusters

3 White-Note Clusters (IV from *32 Piano Games*)

♩ = 80   Ross Lee Finney (United States, b. 1906)

Technique Exercises

Play all the exercises in the major patterns of C, G, D, A, F, E, and B.

Exercise 1: Independent Hands and Hands Coordination   Review Exercise 2 on p. 56 before playing this one. This exercise, like the one on p. 56, is in two parts. Part A features the RH rhythmically moving in shorter durations against the longer durations of the LH. Part B reverses this rhythmic movement. Practice hands together and with each hand separately. Play legato, allowing only one note to sound at a time. Let the weight of your arm shift from one finger to the next while you keep a good hand position and a flexible wrist.

Part A

Part B

Exercise 2: Hand Position Shift   In this Bartók study, you will shift from the G major five-finger pattern to the D major pattern and then return to the G pattern. Practice this hand position shift, trying not to look down at the keys.

Study: **Changing Hand Position** (from *First Term at the Piano*)

Moderato   Béla Bartók (Hungary, 1881–1945)

Chapter Evaluation

1. Perform with rhythmic accuracy the following pieces, which include anacrusis, dotted notes, or both: "Minuet 10" (excerpt) by Haydn, p. 61, and "English Folk Melody 2," p. 63.

2. Play major triads constructed on the tonic of the following major five-finger patterns: C, D, E♭, F, A, B♭. Perform in block-chord and broken-chord forms.

3. Transpose any melody in this chapter to another major five-finger pattern.

4. Perform by memory one of the pieces in this chapter.

5. Demonstrate hand position shift by performing the "Study: Changing Hand Position" by Bartók on p. 76.

6. Circle the anacrusis (upbeat) in the following example. Indicate on what beat the upbeat begins.

The Star-Spangled Banner (excerpt)

John Stafford Smith (England, 1750–1836)
Francis Scott Key (United States, 1779–1843)

7. For each dotted note, write the equivalent notes.

8. Write the designated major triads. When accidentals are needed, write the sharps or the flats on the staff *before* the notes.

9. Notate the A major five-finger pattern in the treble and bass clefs. Construct the tonic (I) chord on the staff at right.

10. Two paired phrases that are almost identical are described as being _____ . Describe contrasting phrases.

❖ Five

Minor Five-Finger Pattern

Minor Triad

Extension Fingering

❖ MELODY

Minor Five-Finger Pattern

The whole-half step arrangement of the *minor five-finger pattern* (the first five notes of a minor scale) is as follows:

A minor five-finger pattern, like the major one, can be built on any of the twelve keys or pitches. The whole-half step pattern is illustrated on the white keys from A to E.

Playing the Minor Five-Finger Pattern

1. Notate the pitches for the following minor patterns. Follow the whole-half-whole-whole pattern exactly. Play each.

D minor	*G minor*	*C minor*	*E minor*

79

2. Try Technique Exercise 1 in this chapter with the C minor five-finger pattern.

Comparing Major and Minor Five-Finger Patterns

In the minor pattern, the third pitch is the only one that is different from the major pattern. To make a major five-finger pattern minor, lower the third tone a half step.

C major   *C minor*

Playing Major and Minor Patterns

To hear and understand the contrast between the major and minor patterns, play the following exercise. Transpose the exercise to the five-finger patterns of G, D, A, F, E, and B.

C major / C minor

Intervals

In the minor five-finger pattern, the interval of the third is the only one that is different from the major pattern. The *minor third* is a half step smaller than the major third.

Intervals in the Minor Five-Finger Pattern

C minor

Interval Exercises

1. Read and play each interval in the minor five-finger pattern. Feel the distances and listen to the sound of each interval.

2. Play these intervals in the following pattern. Stress independent finger action, and work for a legato sound. Transpose to other minor five-finger patterns.

Minor Five-Finger Interval Exercise

C minor

3. Practice major and minor thirds in Technique Exercise 2 in this chapter.

Performing Minor Five-Finger Melodies

Sight-read the following minor melodies after visually analyzing each. Determine the minor pattern by checking the last note of the melody. Play the pattern in ascending and descending form. Check the meter, and clap and count the rhythm of the melody. Keep your eyes on the music, not on your hands. Feel the interval relationships between notes.

Czechoslovakian Folk Melody 1

Moderato

Transpose to E minor

Melody

Moderato

Ferdinand Beyer (1803–1863)

Adagio

Daniel Gottlob Türk (Germany, 1750–1813)

In the excerpt from "Riders on the Storm," a tie is introduced. A **tie** ($\overset{\frown}{\downarrow\,\downarrow}$) connects two identical notes and indicates that they should be performed as a single note. *Play the first note only*, and hold it through the time value of the second note.

Riders on the Storm (excerpt)

Jim Morrison (United States, 1943–1971)

Ri - ders on the storm, ri - ders on the storm, in

to this house we're born, in - to this world we're thrown.

German Folk Melody 3

Andante

mf

Transpose to A minor

Eric Canal (excerpt)

Adagio

American Folk Song

p *f* *p*

f

Transpose to F minor

❖ **HARMONY**

Major and Minor Triads

The only pitch that is different in parallel major and minor triads is the middle one. To change a major triad to a minor triad, lower the middle pitch a half step. In lead sheet notation, a capital letter followed by a lowercase *m* indicates a minor chord.

C major triad

C minor triad

Performing Major and Minor Triads

1. Perform the following major and minor triad exercise. Feel the lowered third in the minor triad.

Major and Minor Triad Exercise

2. Practice major and minor five-finger patterns and triads in Technique Exercise 3 in this chapter.

Minor Triad

The **minor triad** includes a *minor third* (three half steps) between the root and the third, a *major third* (four half steps) between the third and the fifth, and a *perfect fifth* (seven half steps) between the root and the fifth.

A minor triad

D minor triad

Performing Minor Triads in Block-Chord Form

Practice the minor triad in *block-chord form* in the following positions at the keyboard. Use the hand-over-hand technique when specified, and strive for a legato sound between chords. Try these positions with other minor triads.

Block-Chord Exercise: Minor Triad

Part A

Part B

Performing Minor Triads in Arpeggio Form

Practice the minor triad in the broken-chord, or arpeggio, form. Again, connect chord tones as smoothly as you can. Try these positions with different minor triads.

Arpeggio Exercise: Minor Triad

Part A

Part B

Tonic Chord

The first pitch of the minor five-finger pattern is called the tonic, and the chord built on the first step is called the *tonic chord* or i. The tonic chord for the minor pattern is a minor triad. (Lowercase roman numerals are often used for minor triads.)

D minor five-finger pattern—Tonic chord

Tonic Chord and Minor Five-Finger Pattern

Locate the tonic triad for each minor five-finger pattern. Play the following exercise in these minor five-finger patterns: D, A, E; and C, G, F.

D minor

Performing Melodies with Minor Triad Accompaniment

The following minor melodies are accompanied with the minor triad or use the minor triad as part of the accompaniment. Analyze each before playing. Determine the minor pattern and triad; then play both. Notice the interval relationship between notes. Be sure to keep your eyes on the music.

Bulgarian Folk Melody

Allegro

Transpose to G minor

Folk Melody 7

Adagio

Transpose to D minor

Israeli Folk Melody 2

Moderato

Transpose to F minor

Polish Folk Melody

Transpose to E minor

❖ RHYTHM

Rhythm Exercise: Clap, chant, or play the following examples on any key(s), or any chord. Check the number of beats per measure and the number of beats or fraction of beats each note and rest receive.

Composing Project

Compose a melody in parallel phrase structure. Use only the pitches in the F minor triad, and conclude the melody on the F pitch. Decide whether a drone or an F minor triad could be used for accompaniment. Divide the melody equally between the hands. Notate your composition, and prepare to perform.

Ensemble Playing

Duet Exercise 42*

Piano 1 (Students)

Andante

Ferdinand Beyer (1803–1863)

Piano 2 (Teacher)

Andante

---

*To perform with two students at one piano, one student plays Piano 1 as written while another plays Piano 1 two octaves lower.

The "Middle Eastern Folk Melody" may be performed by two pianists or two groups of pianists* as follows:

Piano 1   Perform this ostinato for a two-measure introduction, throughout the piece, and as a two-measure coda (ending).

Ostinato

Piano 2   Play the "Middle Eastern Folk Melody" beginning after Piano 1's two-measure introduction.

Middle Eastern Folk Melody

---

*Two pianists seated at one piano could perform Piano 1 and 2 parts with one performer on the Piano 1 part (an octave lower than written) and the other on Piano 2 (an octave higher than written).

Repertoire

Visually analyze the following pieces. What can you say about the intervals between pitches? Are there definite phrases? If so, are they parallel, contrasting, or something different? What about the tempo and the dynamics? Look up information about Van de Vate in Biographical Sketches of *PianoLab* Composers (Appendix M) and Van de Vate's and Kunz's places in the history of music in the Timeline (Appendix K). Choose one of the pieces to memorize.

"A Quiet Exchange" falls within an E-to-B white-note five-finger pattern. This pattern is not major or minor but part of the Phrygian mode (see Chapter 10). Notice how the material in the first four measures appears in opposite hands in the second four measures (called *invertible counterpoint*). Move the RH up one octave when repeating this piece. Play as softly as possible.

A Quiet Exchange

Moderato   Nancy Van de Vate (United States, b. 1930)

© 1988, Nancy Van de Vate. Used by Permission. All Rights Reserved.

In "Canon,"* notice the imitation of the RH melody in the LH. This piece falls within the E minor five-finger pattern. Practice hands separately and then hands together.

Canon

Konrad Max Künz (Germany, 1812–1875)

---
*A **canon** is a composition in which all parts have the same melody, but start at different times.

Technique Exercises

Check your keyboard position and your hand position.

Exercise 1: Contrary Motion   Keep your wrists flexible and your arms moving in a gentle outward and upward movement for each two-measure pattern in Part A. When you arrive at the whole note, look ahead to what comes next so you'll be ready. In Part B, the arm movements will be reversed. Transpose this exercise to the minor patterns of G, A, D, E, B, and F.

Part A

Part B

Exercise 2: Consecutive Thirds   Practice this exercise slowly with each hand separately and with both hands together. Connect the thirds as smoothly as possible. Change to other major and minor patterns.

Exercise 3: Parallel Motion   The major and minor five-finger patterns and major and minor triads are explored in this exercise. Be attentive to independent finger action on the major and minor pattern. Transpose to the major and parallel minor patterns of G, A, D, E, B, and F.

Exercise 4: Extension Fingering   The five-finger pattern is extended to cover six pitches instead of five in this major and minor exercise. Play without accidentals (in parentheses) for the C major pattern and with accidentals for the C minor pattern. Practice for clarity and accuracy. Transpose to other major and minor patterns.

Chapter Evaluation

1. Build and play a minor five-finger pattern on the following tonics: C, D, E, F, and G.

2. Using the A minor pattern, play major seconds, minor thirds, and perfect fourths and fifths.

3. At the keyboard, transpose "Czechoslovakian Folk Melody 1" on p. 82 from D minor to C minor.

4. Demonstrate a minor triad on any given root, and identify the minor third and the perfect fifth. Contrast a major triad with a minor triad at the keyboard.

5. Perform by memory one of the pieces in this chapter.

6. Demonstrate extension fingering by performing Technique Exercise 4 in this chapter.

7. The whole-half step arrangement of the minor five-finger pattern is as follows:

   1 ___(whole)___ 2 _____ 3 _____ 4 _____ 5

8. Notate the following minor five-finger patterns on the staff and keyboard chart. When accidentals are needed, write the sharps or the flats on the staff *before* the pitches on the *same* line or in the *same* space.

9. Label the following intervals by quality and number (for example, m3). Underneath this identification, specify the number of half steps in each interval. Use the preceding keyboard charts to help in visualizing the half steps.

10. Write minor triads on the following roots.

❖ Six

Major Scales

Major Key Signatures

Tonic and Dominant Chords

Crossover/Crossunder Fingering

Thumb-Under Technique

Staccato Touch

❖ MELODY

Introduction to Scales

The word **scale** comes from the Latin word *scala*, meaning ladder. In music of Western civilization, scales can be identified by particular interval patterns. The two scale forms most familiar to us are the *major* and the *minor scales*, but the pentatonic, whole-tone, blues, and many other scales and modes also serve as the pitch framework for much of the world's music.

The Major Scale

The pattern of the **major scale** includes five whole steps and two half steps.

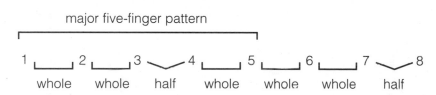

The major scale pattern is illustrated by the white keys on the keyboard from C to C.

C major scale

Performing the C Major Scale

1. Say or sing the letter names as you play the C major scale. Use the **tetra-chord** (succession of four pitches), or two-handed, fingering. Notice the important pull of the seventh step (B) toward the eighth step (C).

C major scale

2. Play the descending C major scale at the beginning of "Joy to the World."

Joy to the World (excerpt)

Isaac Watts
George Frideric Handel (Germany, 1685–1759)

Joy   to   the world,   the   Lord   is   come;

3. Play "St. Paul's Steeple" using the tetrachord fingering. (Play also as a **round** with four groups, each group starting after the first two notes of the previous group.

St. Paul's Steeple

American Folk Melody

The major scale without alterations is referred to as **diatonic.** Major scales may begin on any of the twelve available pitches, and as long as the whole-half step pattern (the diatonic pattern) is reproduced exactly, the characteristic sound will be the same. The only major scale that has no sharps or flats is C.

Examples:

G major scale　　　　　　　　　　　　　　　　*F major scale*

Performing Major Scales

1. Play the G major and F major scales just given with tetrachord fingering.
2. Perform the following major scale tetrachord exercise. This exercise will help you learn the major scale patterns with sharps. Begin with the C major scale two octaves below middle C, and play in tetrachord position. Then place your LH on the upper tetrachord of the C major scale (G A B C), making this the lower tetrachord of the G major scale. Remember to cover the RH notes quickly with the LH. (Notice that your RH fourth finger always plays the new sharp.)

Major Scale Tetrachord Exercise: Sharp Keys

C major　　　　　*G major*　　　　　*D major*　　　　　*A major*

3. Perform the following major scale tetrachord exercise with scales that include flats. Begin with the Cb major scale (two octaves below middle C) and play in tetrachord position. Again place your LH on the upper tetrachord of the Cb major scale (Gb Ab Bb Cb), making this the lower tetrachord of the Gb major scale. Notice that your RH fourth finger always "drops" a flat from the previous scale.

Major Scale Tetrachord Exercise: Flat Keys

Identification of Scale Tones

Scale Degrees

Each pitch, or degree, of the major scale has a specific name.

Major scale degrees

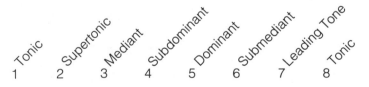

Syllable Names

Pitches may be identified by letters, numbers, degree names, and *syllable names*. Seven syllable names—do, re, mi, fa, sol, la, ti—are often used to identify pitches in a scale.

C major scale and syllables

In the song "Do-Re-Mi" from the musical *The Sound of Music*, syllables are used as part of the lyrics. Sing the syllable names while playing the scale sequence in the final measures of "Do-Re-Mi."

Do-Re-Mi (excerpt)

Oscar Hammerstein II (United States, 1895–1960)
Richard Rodgers (United States, 1902–1979)

Major Key Signatures

The sharps or the flats needed to create the various major scales are placed at the beginning of each staff of music (right after the clef sign). This grouping of the sharps and flats is called a **key signature.**

Any sharp or flat in the key signature applies to the corresponding note in all octaves. For example, if a B-flat is in the key signature, then all B's (whether in bass or treble clef or in any position on the staff) must be performed as B-flats.

Placement of Sharps and Flats

The sharps and the flats in the key signature are placed in a specific order. The order of sharps is F C G D A E B.

The order of flats is B E A D G C F. Notice that the order of flats is the reverse of the order of sharps.

Guidelines for Determining the Tonic or Major Key

In a key signature of sharps, the sharp farthest to the right is scale tone 7. The next line or space above (one half step above) is the key or the tonic.

Sharp key signatures

There are two ways to determine the tonic in a key signature of flats. First, the next-to-the-last flat is the tonic. (You have to memorize that the key of F has one flat.) Second, the flat farthest to the right is scale tone 4. Count down to 1 (the tonic).

Flat key signatures

Circle of Fifths

The fifteen major scales and key signatures can be arranged in a sequence called the **circle of fifths.** Moving clockwise *up* the interval of a perfect fifth to the tonic, you can see that each new key adds one more sharp. Moving counter-clockwise *down* a perfect fifth, you can see that each key adds one more flat. Three keys are enharmonic: B and C♭, F♯ and G♭, and C♯ and D♭.

The circle of fifths (major keys)

Enharmonic Keys

Identifying Major Keys

Determine the major key for the following pieces. Since most pieces usually end
on the tonic, identify that pitch. Also determine the tonic by means of the key
signature. (You must learn these either by memorization or by using the guidelines presented earlier in this chapter.) Carefully analyze the melody, rhythm,
and form; then perform each piece.

Wiegenlied   Daniel Gottlob Türk (Germany, 1750–1813)

Hush Little Baby   American Folk Song

Intervals

There are eight different intervals created between the tonic and the eight ascending degrees of the major scale. The seconds, thirds, sixths, and sevenths are always major intervals; the unisons, fourths, fifths, and octaves are always perfect.

Intervals in Major Scale

C major

Interval Exercises

1. Read and play each interval in the major scale. Feel the distances and listen to the sound of each interval.

2. Play these intervals in the following exercise. Stress independent finger action, and work for a legato sound. Transpose to other major scales.

Major Scale Interval Exercise

C major

Major Scale (One-Hand Fingering)

To play a major scale with one hand, you must cross fingers over and under other fingers. The major scales are fingered in several ways. One-hand fingerings for all major scales are in Appendix D. The fingering for the C major scale (also the same for the G, D, A, and E scales) is as follows:

C major scale

Performing Major Scales (One-Hand Fingering)

1. Practice the following thumb-under exercise in preparation for one-hand scale playing. In this exercise, the thumb will tuck under to move as smoothly as possible to the next pitch. The thumb needs to do all the work; the hands and arms stay relaxed and without movement. Play this exercise hands separately first and then hands together. Continue the pattern until you reach the upper C.

Thumb-Under Exercise in Major

2. Practice the C major scale with one-hand fingering in two octaves in contrary motion. Practice hands separately, then hands together. Notice that the fingering is the same in the two hands.

C major scale in contrary motion

3. Practice the C major scale with one-hand fingering in two octaves in parallel motion (p. 107).

4. Once the fingering is secure for the C major scale, try the G and D major scales in contrary motion and in parallel motion.

G major scale

D major scale

5. Practice Technique Exercise 1 in this chapter.

Performing Major Scale Melodies (One-Hand Fingering)

1. This South American folk melody uses all the pitches in the major scale. Use the one-hand fingering with the RH. What is the range of the LH part?

South American Melody

2. "The First Noel" is a more challenging scale melody. Practice the RH one-hand fingering. Look only at the music, even when your thumb moves under. Feel the movement. Perform by yourself or with another pianist.

(One pianist can play the RH melody while another plays the bass line. At one piano, a pianist can play the bass line as written with the LH or the RH while another plays the melody an octave higher.)

The First Noel   Carol

3. For even more challenging scale melodies, try "Joy to the World," p. 263, and the excerpt from "Hymne" by Vangelis, p. 256.

❖ **HARMONY**

Tonic and Dominant Chords

The most important chord in the scale is the tonic (I), and second in importance is the **dominant** or V. In a major scale, both the I and the V are major chords. The tonic triad includes pitches 1, 3, and 5 of the major scale, and the dominant triad includes pitches 5, 7, and 2.

C major scale—I and V chords

Authentic Cadence

Since I conveys the strongest sense of arrival, most melodies conclude on the tonic pitch or chord. Because two of the pitches (7 and 2 of the major scale) in the V chord have a tendency to "pull" toward the I, the V is often followed by the I. When a phrase, section, or piece concludes with the V–I progression, the closing, or **cadence,** is called **authentic.**

Authentic cadence

Op. 117, No. 10

Con moto   Cornelius Gurlitt (Germany, 1820–1901)

*A dot above or below a notehead indicates that the tones should be disconnected and shortened.
See Technique Exercise 2 at the end of the chapter.

Dominant Seventh Chord

The dominant (V) chord is not always a triad. Quite often it includes four notes and is called a **dominant seventh chord** (V7).* The V7 is represented in lead sheet notation by a capital letter plus a 7—for example, C7, G7, F7.

To simplify the finger and hand moves between the I and V7 chords, one of the tones (the fifth) of the V7 chord is often omitted and the others are rearranged or inverted. This is often called the *piano position*. The top notes in the two chords stay the same while the middle note of the dominant seventh chord moves up a half step and the bottom note moves down a half step.

The RH fingering of the **V7** chord in piano position is $\frac{5}{4}$.

The LH fingering of the **V7** chord in piano position is $\frac{1}{2}$.

---

*More information on seventh chords is found in Chapter 8.

I and V7 Chords in Selected Major Keys

Practice the I and the V7 chords in the following frequently used major keys (all chords and fingerings are in Appendix G). Develop a feel for this progression and be ready to change chords.

Key of C major

Key of D major

Key of F major

Performing I–V7 Chords

1. Perform the following exercise to practice the necessary moves between the two chords. Part A prepares the hands for the moves between the two chords in Part B. Transpose this exercise to all major keys.

I–V7 Exercise

Part A

Part B

2. Perform the following pieces using the I and the V7 chords. Review the rhythm, melody, and form of each before playing.

The Cuckoo

German Folk Song

Transpose to D major

English Folk Melody 3

Transpose to A major

Andante   August Eberhard Müller (Germany, 1767–1817)

Other melodies to accompany with I and the V7 chords:

"Little River," p. 51   "Jim-Along Josie," p. 51
"Israeli Folk Melody 1," p. 70   "Chilean Folk Melody," p. 52

Composing Project

Create a two-phrase melody that uses the pitches in the I and the V (or V7) chords of the major key of your choice. Unify your composition with repetition, and incorporate contrasting ideas for variety. Use the following chords for the eight measures. An accompaniment could include chord roots, block chords, broken chords, or any member of the chord. Notate and perform.

Phrase 1:   I | V or V7 | I | V or V7 |
Phrase 2:   I | V or V7 | V or V7 | I   ‖

Ensemble Playing

Etude, Op. 82, No. 10

Piano 1   Cornelius Gurlitt (Germany, 1820–1901)

Etude, Op. 82, No. 11

Piano 2

Cornelius Gurlitt (Germany, 1820–1901)

"Come, Follow" may be performed as a round with three groups of pianists.

Come, Follow

John Hilton (England, 1599–1657)
arr. Linda Mankin

Lively

Repertoire

Analyze each of the following pieces. Choose at least one to memorize. Look up
information about the composers (Appendix M) and their places in the history of
music (Appendix K).

Eighteenth-century composers generally did not include touch, dynamic markings, and the like in their music. But the touch for "March" (Türk) would most likely be the "normal" one of the eighteenth century—*non legato*. Türk indicates in his *Klavierschule* book (1789) that "for those notes which are to be played in the normal touch, one lifts each finger off the key a bit earlier than the actual note values may indicate."

March
                                                          Daniel Gottlob Türk (Germany, 1750–1813)

In the Gurlitt composition, a dialogue between the RH and the LH is featured. Practice in four-measure segments hands together.

Study for Two

Con moto
                                                          Cornelius Gurlitt (Germany, 1820–1901)

A **duet** is usually a composition to be performed by two people. This piece is a "duet" for just one person; actually, the duet is performed by the player's left and right hands.

A Duet (No. 2 from *First Term at the Piano*)

Moderato   Béla Bartók (Hungary, 1881–1945)

Technique Exercises

Exercise 1: Thumb-Under   This thumb-under exercise requires the thumb to tuck under several fingers. Again, try to move as smoothly as possible. Keep the hand in position, and keep the hands and arms relaxed. Make the thumb do all the work. Play this exercise in many different major patterns.

Staccato Touch

Staccato touch requires playing in a detached style. In notation, the staccato mark (♩ or ♪) appears above or below the notehead to indicate that the tones should be disconnected and shortened. Staccato playing is the opposite of legato playing.

To get a feel for the wrist action important in staccato touch, knock with your knuckles on the keyboard lid or the top of the piano. Be sure to knock with your wrist loose and your arm not moving. Once this knocking action is secure, tap first with your index finger (2), gradually adding the middle (3) and ring (4) fingers.

Exercise 2: Staccato Touch   Transfer this knocking wrist action to the keyboard by playing the following examples hands separately with the staccato touch. Strike each key with a precise motion from the wrist only. Release the key immediately. Keep your wrist loose but your arm still.

Part A

Part B

Chapter Evaluation

1. Demonstrate the major scale pattern and key signatures by playing the tetrachord exercises in this chapter.

2. At the keyboard, transpose "St. Paul's Steeple" (earlier in this chapter) from C major to D major.

3. Using the C major scale, play and identify these intervals: major second, major third, perfect fourth, perfect fifth, major sixth, major seventh, and perfect octave.

4. Demonstrate the one-hand fingering (two octaves) for the G major scale.

5. Play I and V7 chords (with the V7 rearranged in "piano position") in any major key. Demonstrate smooth hand shifts.

6. Perform one of the pieces in the Repertoire section accurately and musically. Be able to discuss the characteristics of its melody, rhythm, and form.

7. Write the whole-half step arrangement of the major scale:

   1 (whole) 2 _____ 3 _____ 4 _____ 5 _____ 6 _____ 7 _____ 8

8. Construct major scales, ascending and descending, on the following tonics. Write the letter name, the number, and the syllable (do, re, and so on) under each pitch. When accidentals are needed, write the sharps or the flats *before* the pitches on the *same* line or in the *same* space.

9. Identify the following scale degrees by letter name.
   a. The tonic of the E♭ major scale is _____ .
   b. The dominant of the F major scale is _____ .
   c. The leading tone of the D major scale is _____ .
   d. The subdominant of the G major scale is _____ .
   e. The supertonic of the B♭ major scale is _____ .
   f. The mediant of the A major scale is _____ .
   g. The submediant of the C major scale is _____ .

10. Notate the tonic for each major key as determined by the key signature.

11. Write the key signatures for the designated keys. Be sure that the flats and
   the sharps are in the correct order, are in the appropriate lines or spaces,
   and are not crowded. Refer to the key signature chart on p. 102.

12. Complete the following.
   a. The key of F major has _____ flats.
   b. The key of D major has _____ sharps.
   c. The key of E major has _____ sharps.
   d. The key of B♭ major has _____ flats.
   e. The key of A major has _____ sharps.
   f. The key of E♭ major has _____ flats.
   g. The key of G major has _____ sharps.

13. Label the following intervals by quality and number.

14. Construct the tonic (I) and the dominant (V or V7) chords on the appropriate scale degrees.

Seven

Primary Chords

Twelve-Bar Blues Progression

Syncopation

A B and A B A Form

Legato Pedaling

Drop/Lift Technique

❖ HARMONY

Primary Chords

The I (tonic) and the V (dominant) chords were presented in Chapter 6. By adding the IV (subdominant) chord, we have identified the **primary chords.** These are the three most frequently used chords in tonal music.

The **subdominant** chord is built on the fourth degree of the scale and, like the I and V chords, is a major triad in a major key. The IV chord includes pitches 4, 6, and 8 (1) of the major scale.

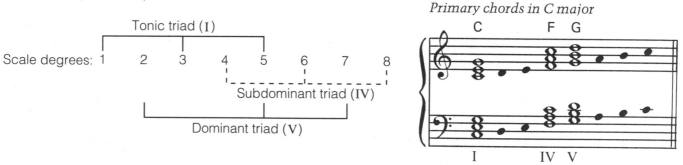

Primary chords in C major

Plagal Cadence

The tonic triad is always the last chord in a final cadence. When the tonic triad is preceded by a subdominant chord, the result is a **plagal cadence** (IV–I).

Plagal cadence

Tar Paper Stomp*

Wingy Manone (United States, b. 1904)

plagal cadence

Performing Primary Chords

1. Practice the following exercise, which changes between these three chords. Play in the designated block-chord form and in arpeggio form. Transpose to other major scales.

Block Chord Exercise: I–IV–V

*The big band hit "In the Mood" was based on "Tar Paper Stomp."

2. Practice Technique Exercise 2 at the end of this chapter. Try the technique described there with the preceding Block Chord Exercise. Hold the pedal down until a new chord is indicated.

3. Perform the chords in "Tar Paper Stomp" with your LH while the instructor or more experienced players perform the RH melody. Notice that the entire melody consists of pitches in each of the three chords.

Twelve-Bar Blues Progression

The traditional twelve-bar **blues** (twelve measures) can be played using the primary chords. The chord order for one version of the twelve-bar progression follows.

    I I I   IV IV I I   V IV I I

Practice the blues progression in C major. At first you might play just the root of each chord; then play all the pitches in the chords. Develop a feel for the distances so you do not have to look down at the keys. Bring RH 1 to RH 5; LH 5 to LH 1 quickly when moving from the I chord to the V chord. Reverse the process in moving from V to I.

Twelve-bar blues progression

To create a RH melody based on the blues progression, you can play the tones in each chord one at a time. Practice "Chordal Melody" looking at the music, not at your hands. Continue to feel these chord jumps. When you are comfortable with the piece, vary the rhythm and the order of chord tones to create a new version.

Finally, transpose "Chordal Melody" to primary chords in other major keys.

Chordal Melody

Performing Blues Compositions

1. "Plain Blues" incorporates **blue notes** (lowered thirds of each chord). (The natural sign—♮—cancels a flat or a sharp.) Use the same fingering for each chord. Notice the *accent marks* (>) on beat two in each measure—stress this note and a more "bluesy" flavor will result.

Plain Blues

Transpose to B♭ major

2. In "Leftie Blues," the LH plays the individual chord tones and blue notes
    (an octave lower than written), while the RH plays the block chords. No-
    tice the accent mark on beat two—again, observe the result.

Leftie Blues

Transpose to B♭ major

3. "Amanda's Blues" features a steady eighth-note rhythm in the RH. Keep
    your wrist loose as you perform the eighth notes. The LH "walks" through
    the chord tones and the blues notes an octave lower than written.

Amanda's Blues

Amanda Hebert

8va sempre

(8va sempre)

(8va sempre)

Transpose to B♭ major

© 1980, Amanda Hebert. Used by permission.

> Amanda Hebert composed this blues piece while enrolled in a beginning piano and music fundamentals course at San Francisco State University.

4. More blues pieces may be found on pp. 140, 247, and 248.

❖ RHYTHM

Syncopation

Syncopation is a rhythmic device that gives variety and interest to all kinds of music. It is integral to the blues as well as to other forms of American jazz. It also occurs in the music of many cultures.

   Syncopation is the placement of accents on normally unaccented beats or unaccented parts of beats. It may be likened to putting an accent on the wrong syllable in language. The effect of this shifting of accents is that the rhythm of the melody does not coincide with the steady beat.

In "Plain Blues" (p. 125) and "Leftie Blues" on p. 126, beat two (normally a weak beat) was accented throughout, creating syncopation: $\frac{4}{4}$ ♩ ♩ ♩ ♩ |.

Syncopation may also be achieved by omitting an accent where one is expected as well as by placing one where it is not expected. When a rest is placed on a strong beat, the accent is shifted to a weak beat: $\frac{4}{4}$ 𝄾 ♩ ♩♩ ♩ |.

Rhythm Exercise: Syncopation—accented offbeats, omitted accents (rests)

Performing Syncopated Melodies

"Shabat, Shalom" includes accents on offbeats to create syncopation. Clap the rhythm of the melody before playing. The RH part falls within the D minor five-finger pattern (D E F G A).

Shabat, Shalom (excerpt)

Hebrew Song

Sha-bat, sha- lom,   sha-bat, sha- lom,   sha-bat, sha | lom, sha-bat, sha

lom, sha - | lom!

In measures 3, 4, and 7 of "Creole Dance," quarter rests are placed on the customary first-beat accent. Determine the major key, and clap the rhythm of the melody before performing.

Creole Dance

Other melodies in major keys that include syncopated rhythms:

"Hey Lidee," p. 262

"Tom Dooley," p. 147

"Hello! Ma' Baby," p. 132

❖ FORM

Sectional Form

In longer pieces of music, phrases are combined and organized into *sections*. Some pieces can be divided into two or three sections. Pieces with two sections are referred to as *two-part* (**A B**) or **binary form,** whereas three-section pieces are **ternary** (**A B A**).

A B (Binary) Form

"Dance" is an example of A B, or binary, form. The second section (beginning in measure 9) requires good finger action with the RH. Practice this exercise before playing the piece. What is the range of the RH part in this piece?

Dance   Cornelius Gurlitt (Germany, 1820–1901)

A B A (Ternary) Form

"Funny Dialogue" has three sections (A B A). Notice how the rhythmic *motives* (brief musical ideas) ♩ ♫ ♩ and ♫♫♩ are manipulated and used to unify. Clap these rhythms first; then practice a section at a time. This could also be performed with another player (one on RH and one on LH).

Funny Dialogue

Allegretto

Dmitri Kabalevsky (Russia, 1904–1987)

Determine the formal design (A B or A B A) for the following pieces:

"Bourreé by L. Mozart, p. 234   "We Three Kings," p. 185

"Mazurka" by Szymanowska, p. 243   "Hey Lidee," p. 262

Composing Projects

1. Create a piano blues piece based on the twelve-bar progression. Notate both LH and RH parts. Incorporate blue notes, syncopation, and, possibly, **grace notes** (a short note, printed in small type, which ornaments the following note). See grace notes in pieces on pp. 238, 243, and 248.

2. Create a boogie-woogie based on the standard twelve-bar blues progression. Use one of the boogie bass lines in Appendix H.

Ensemble Playing

Hello! Ma' Baby

Joseph E. Howard (United States, 1878–1961)
Ida Emerson (United States, late 19th–20th c.)

Piano 1

Piano 2

Razzle Dazzle

Piano 1 (Students)

Moderate swing

Lee Evans (United States, b. 1933)

Piano 2 (Teacher)

Moderate swing

Repertoire

Study the Bartók piece and identify the five-finger pattern used in both hands. Does the first phrase use parallel or contrary motion between hands? Notice the legato and staccato markings. Practice Technique Exercise 3 in this chapter before playing the piece.

Morning Song (No. 5 from *First Term at the Piano*)

Moderato

Béla Bartók (Hungary, 1881–1945)

What do you notice about phrases 1 and 2 in "Up or Out"? Note the change in dynamics and the register change of the RH in phrase 2.

Up or Out

Moderato

Nancy Van de Vate (United States, b. 1930)

What is the sectional form for this Beethoven piece? What can you say about the phrases? Practice one section at a time.

Russian Folk Song, Op. 107, No. 3   Ludwig van Beethoven (Germany, 1770–1827)

Technique Exercises

Exercise 1: Independent Hands and Hand Coordination   Establish a good hand position. Practice this exercise with good finger action. Feel the weight of your arm shift from one finger to the next. Connect pitches as smoothly as possible. Transpose to other major keys.

Pedaling

When the **damper pedal** (located to the far right) is pressed down, pitches can be sustained to produce a legato effect. This depressing of the pedal releases the felt dampers from the strings and permits the strings to vibrate freely. (Look inside the piano to see what happens when you play a note and depress the damper pedal.)

To use the damper pedal, rest the ball of the foot lightly on the pedal, keeping your heel on the floor. Practice depressing and releasing the pedal. Check that your heel does not leave the floor. Listen for any mechanical noises—you should pedal with as little noise as possible. A marking in music for the damper pedal is as follows:

down   up-down   up

Play a note, depress the damper pedal, then remove your finger from the key. Listen to the continuing sound. Repeat this exercise until you can smoothly and quickly play a note and immediately depress the pedal.

Exercise 2: Legato Pedaling   To legato-pedal, you must learn to connect several notes or chords with the pedal. To do this, you must play a note, depress the pedal, play another note releasing the pedal, and immediately depress again.

Try this exercise connecting one pitch to the next without a break. Listen carefully to make sure the pedal has sustained only one note. Clear pedaling is the goal.

down   up-down

Perform the primary chords in C major adding the legato pedaling. Transpose the primary chords to other major keys.

Exercise 3: Drop/Lift   Practice these two-note slurs with action mainly from the wrist. Elevate the wrist a bit, and as you play the first note, drop the wrist to key level with a slight bounce. On the second note, lift the wrist to the original position. Keep your fingers firm. Transpose to other major keys.

Chapter Evaluation

1. Play I, IV, and V chords (in root position) in the keys of C, G, D, F, and B♭.

2. At the keyboard, improvise a blueslike piece using primary chords in the twelve-bar blues progression.

3. Demonstrate legato pedaling with the primary chords in Technique Exercise 2 in this chapter, or in the I–IV–V exercise earlier in the chapter.

4. Demonstrate understanding of syncopation by performing one of the lines in the rhythm exercise in this chapter.

5. Memorize and perform a piece in A B or A B A form.

6. Write the I, IV, and V chords (in root position) for the following major keys.

7. Identify the primary chords by letter name for the twelve-bar blues progression in B♭ major.

I (____)   I (____)   I (____)   I (____)

IV (____)   IV (____)   I (____)   I (____)

V (____)   IV (____)   I (____)   I (____)

8. Notate possible pitches for a melody line as indicated by the LH chords in each measure.

9. _____ is the placing of emphasis on normally weak beats or weak parts of beats.

10. A musical composition that includes *two* contrasting sections is known as _____ or _____ form, and one with *three* sections is known as _____ or _____ form.

❖ Eight

Dominant Seventh Chord

Chord Inversions/Figured Bass

Nonchord Tones

Harmonization

Compound Meter

Alberti Bass

❖ HARMONY

Seventh Chord

The **seventh chord** includes four notes: a triad with an added third. There are several kinds of seventh chords, but the one frequently used in *PianoLab* is the *major-minor seventh chord*. This chord, also commonly referred to as the **dominant seventh chord**, includes a major triad with an added seventh above the root.

Major-minor (dominant) seventh chord

Performing Major-Minor Seventh Chords

"Seventh Chord Blues" and "Seventh Chord Boogie" both include open sevenths (m7) in the LH part. Determine what the other chord tones would be in each of the seventh chords.

Seventh Chord Blues

Seventh Chord Boogie

Chord Inversions

Triads and seventh chords are not always written in root position (the root of the chord positioned as the lowest pitch). Chord tones may be rearranged, or *inverted.*

The triad has two **inversions.**

Root position

1st inversion

2nd inversion

The seventh chord has three **inversions.**

Root position   *1st inversion*   *2nd inversion*   *3rd inversion*

Chord Inversions with Figured Bass

Arabic numerals are sometimes added to roman numerals to indicate specific chord inversions, as in V7. The use of arabic numerals originated in the *figured bass* system of the *Baroque period* (c. 1600–1750), when keyboard players were skilled in improvising elaborate compositions from a given series of pitches and numerals (figures).

The numerals show intervals within the chord and are measured from the lowest (bass) note to the other notes in the chord. Parentheses identify numbers not commonly shown but understood to be in the chord.

Figures for triads

Triad	Arabic numerals
Root	none
1st inversion	6
2nd inversion	$^6_4$

(5)   6   6
(3) (3) 4

Figures for seventh chords

Seventh chord	Arabic numerals
Root	7
1st inversion	$^6_5$
2nd inversion	$^4_3$
3rd inversion	$^4_2$

7   6   (6)   (6)
(5) 5   4   4
(3) (3)   3   2

Chord Inversions for Keyboard Playing

To make the hand and finger moves easier between two or three chords, some chords are performed in inversions. These inversions allow the hand to stay in one position and play two or three chords.

I and IV⁶₄ Chords

Of the two inversions of the IV triad, the second inversion (IV⁶₄) is the closer to the tonic (I) in root position. Notice how the bottom notes stay the same for the two chords while the middle note moves up a half step and the top note moves up a whole step.

I and IV$_4^6$ Chords in Selected Major Keys

| C major | G major | D major | A major | F major | Bb major | Eb major |

Performing I–IV$_4^6$ Chords

1. Perform Part A of the following exercise, which prepares the hands for the I–IV$_4^6$–I fingerings.

2. Perform Part B of the I–IV$_4^6$ Exercise to practice the necessary moves between the two chords. Transpose to other major keys.

I–IV$_4^6$ Exercise

Part A

Part B

3. Perform "Lovely Evening" using these chords for an accompaniment. First, practice in the usual block-chord style; then try the broken-chord accompaniment shown here.*

Lovely Evening†   Traditional Round

Transpose to F major

4. Practice Technique Exercise 1 at the end of this chapter. This exercise stresses contrary motion and the arpeggio style.

Nonchord Tones

Harmony (chords) and melody are related. For example, in Chapter 7, the melody of "Tar Paper Stomp," p. 123, is made up entirely of pitches in the primary chords, and the blues pieces are based primarily on chord tones.

Although the framework of a melody is mostly chord tones, other pitches are added between them. These tones are called *nonchord tones.*

Passing tones and **neighboring tones** are two kinds of nonchord tones. They often fall on unaccented beats (two and four in quadruple meter; two in duple; and two and three in triple) or on unaccented parts of beats.

Passing tones (p.t.) come between pitches that are a third apart.

---

*Other broken-chord patterns are notated in Appendix H.

†Perform as a round with several groups of pianos. Piano 1 begins the melody. Piano 2 enters when Piano 1 begins measure 7 (2). Piano 3 begins the melody when Piano 2 has reached measure 7. Repeat as many times as desired. (At one piano, one pianist can play Piano 1 part an octave higher while another plays Piano 2 part an octave lower.)

Neighboring tones come stepwise between repeated pitches and can be either upper neighbors (u.n.) or lower neighbors (l.n.).

In the following melody, the I (F) and the V7 (C7) chords serve as the chord framework. The circled pitches are nonchord tones. Label the nonchord tones as p.t. and u.n. or l.n. and perform.

Melody 1

Identifying Nonchord Tones

1. Analyze the following melodies (based on the I and the V7 chords) for nonchord tones. Circle and label the p.t. and u.n. or l.n. Perform each.

   "Whistle Daughter," p. 68   Folk Melody 6, p. 70
   Israeli Folk Melody 1, p. 70   "The Cuckoo," p. 113

2. Add nonchord tones—p.t. and u.n. or l.n.—to the following chordal melody. Place the nonchord tones on unaccented beats or on unaccented parts of beats. Alter the rhythmic durations as needed, and rewrite on the staff below. Perform the melody with chordal accompaniment.

Melody 2

I and V$_5^6$ Chords

In Chapter 6 rearranging the chord tones of the dominant seventh chord (V7) made for a smoother move from the I to the V7. The first inversion (V$_5^6$) is commonly used when playing the I and the V7 because it is the closest to the tonic in root position. Notice how the top notes stay the same for the two chords while the middle note of the V$_5^6$ moves up a half step and the bottom note moves down a half step.

I and V$_5^6$ Chords in Selected Major Keys

Practice the I and the V$_5^6$ chords with the RH and LH in the following frequently used major keys (all chords are in Appendix G). Try to develop a feel for this progression and be ready to change chords.

G major   *D major*   *A major*

Performing I–V⁶₅ Chords

1. Review the I–V7–I exercise on p. 113.
2. Perform the following pieces using the I–V⁶₅ for an accompaniment.

Mary Ann

Calypso Tune

All day, all night Ma-ry Ann,____ Down by the sea-shore, sift-ing sand,____

Sing-ing ev-ery day, oh, Miss Ma-ry Ann,____ Sing ev-ery night, oh, Miss Ma-ry Ann.

Transpose to G major

Tom Dooley

American Folk Song

Hang down your head Tom Doo-ley, Hang down your head and cry.

Transpose to F major

I, IV$^6_4$, and V$^6_5$ Chords in Selected Major Keys*

Key of C major

Key of G major

Key of D major

---

*I, IV, and V7 chords for all major keys are notated in root position and in I–IV$^6_4$–V$^6_5$ form in Appendix G.

Key of A major

A   D   E7

I   IV⁶₄   V⁶₅

Key of E major

E   A   B7

I   IV⁶₄   V⁶₅

Key of F major

F   B♭   C7

I   IV⁶₄   V⁶₅

Key of B♭ major

B♭   E♭   F7

I   IV⁶₄   V⁶₅

Key of E♭ major

Performing I–IV⁶₄–V⁶₅ Chords

1. Perform the following exercise to practice the moves between the three chords. The fingerings and whole-half step moves will be the same in any major key. Memorize this progression. Learn to shift quickly and smoothly from one chord to another. Feel the shape of the next chord, and actually touch the keys just before playing. Transpose this exercise to other major keys.

I–IV⁶₄–V⁶₅ Exercise

2. Use legato or syncopated pedaling for the next exercise of the primary chords. Try not to blur chord tones or overlap sounds of single notes. Connect evenly when crossing hands. Transpose to other major keys.

Arpeggio Exercise: I–IV⁶₄–V⁶₅

3. Perform the following pieces. Determine the major key and the primary chords first; then practice the chord progression. Be sure to review the rhythm, form, fingering, and so on for each piece before performing.

Drink to Me Only with Thine Eyes (excerpt)

English Folk Song

Transpose to F major

Banks of the Ohio

American Ballad

I asked my love to take a walk, To take a walk, a lit-tle walk

And down be-side where the wa-ters flow Down by the banks of the O-hi-o.

Transpose to D major

Amen (excerpt)

Refrain   Black American Spiritual

Transpose to G major

Bohemian Christmas Carol

Transpose to F major

I Never Will Marry

American Folk Song

Transpose to D major

4. The following songs can be accompanied with the I, IV, and V7 chords.

   "The First Noel," p. 109   "Joy to the World," p. 263
   "Amazing Grace," p. 263   "De Colores," p. 266
   "John B," p. 264

Harmonization

Selecting appropriate chords for a melody is referred to as *harmonization*. To select appropriate chords, determine what chord(s) matches pitches in the melody.

Guidelines for Harmonizing Melodies

1. Determine the key of the melody; identify the pitches in the primary chords for that key.

2. For each measure, analyze the pitches in the melody and decide which chord matches the first note and notes on the other strong beats. Many melodies can be harmonized with only one chord per measure. (Pitches in the melody that are not in the chords are nonchord tones.) Keep in mind that a pitch in the melody may be the third, the fifth, or the seventh of a chord, as well as the root. If the melody begins on an anacrusis, the anacrusis is usually not chorded. Remember that a melody normally ends on the tonic, with the tonic chord.

3. Try the chosen chords with the melody. *Always check each musical decision by playing at the keyboard.* Label each measure by chord or chords (roman numeral), and, finally, notate the correct chords (in root position or in the piano position with inversions). "Tante Minna" is an example of such a harmonization.

Tante Minna

Example: C major (I = C E G, V7 = G B D F)   German Folk Melody

Harmonizing Melodies

Harmonize the following melodies. Play the harmonizations, and notate the melodies and the chords on a staff.

The Cradle

Austrian Carol

English Folk Melody 4

French Canadian Round*

Capriccio in G Major (excerpt)

Franz Joseph Haydn (Austria, 1732–1809)

On Top of Old Smoky

American Folk Melody

On top of old Smok - y_____ All cov-ered with snow_____

_____ I lost my true lov - er____ By_ court-ing too slow._____

*Perform "French Canadian Round" with two groups of pianists. Piano 1 begins. Piano 2 enters when Piano 1 has reached measure 3. Repeat as many times as desired. (At one piano, a pianist can perform Piano 1 part an octave higher while another performs Piano 2 an octave lower.)

German Folk Melody 4

Lullaby

Johannes Brahms (Germany, 1833–1897)

Kum Ba Yah

Black American Song

Kum - ba - yah, my Lord, Kum - ba - yah, Kum - ba - yah, my Lord, Kum - ba -

yah, Kum - ba - yah, my Lord, Kum - ba - yah, oh, Lord —— Kum - ba - yah.

❖ RHYTHM

Compound Meters

All the meters studied so far are classified as simple, and in simple meter the beat is divided into two equal parts. When the beat divides into three equal parts, the meter is referred to as **compound.**

Simple

Compound

In compound meter, the beat is represented by a dotted note, which divides into three equal parts. The dotted quarter note (♩.), the dotted half note (♩.), and the dotted whole note (o.) are frequently used beat values.

Selected Compound Meter Signatures

In simple meters, the top number of the meter signature specifies the number of beats per measure and the bottom number identifies the note receiving the beat. Since there is no number to represent a dotted-note beat value, the bottom number of a compound meter signature shows divisions of the beat and the top number shows how many divisions in a measure. The top number is a multiple of three: To determine the meter (duple, triple, quadruple), divide by three.

Compound Duple Meter

6   6 beat divisions per measure   6
8   ♪ is the value of each beat division   8   1 2 3 4 5 6

6   6 beat divisions per measure   6
4   ♩ is the value of each beat division   4   1 2 3 4 5 6

Compound Triple Meter

9   9 beat divisions per measure   9
8   ♪ is the value of each beat division   8   1 2 3 4 5 6 7 8 9

9   9 beat divisions per measure   9
4   ♩ is the value of each beat division   4   1 2 3 4 5 6 7 8 9

Compound Quadruple Meter

12   12 beat divisions per measure   12
8   ♪ is the value of each beat division   8   1 2 3 4 5 6 7 8 9 10 11 12

12   12 beat divisions per measure   12
4   ♩ is the value of each beat division   4   1 2 3 4 5 6 7 8 9 10 11 12

Rhythm Exercise: Compound Meter   Compound meters may be counted several ways. One way is to count the division values of the beat stressing the 1 and 4 (7 and 10). A second way is to say a sound such as "eh" and "ah" on the second and third division of each group of three.

Performing Pieces in Compound Meter

1. Determine the number of beats each note receives, and clap the rhythm of each piece before playing.

Flemish Folk Melody

Transpose to E major

Fiddle Dee Dee

English Folk Melody

Transpose to F major

___

*D.C. al fine (Da capo al fine) means to return to the beginning and conclude with the measure marked *fine*.

Down in the Valley

Kentucky Folk Song

Down in the val - ley, the val -ley so low, Hang your head

o - ver, hear the winds blow, Hear the winds blow, dear, hear the winds

blow, Hang your head o - ver, hear the winds blow.

For He's a Jolly Good Fellow

French Folk Song

fine

D.C. al fine

Transpose to C major

2. For more challenging compound meter examples, perform the following pieces.

"Silent Night," p. 254
"Promenade" (Bielawa), p. 161
"Memory" from *Cats* (excerpt), p. 261
Theme from 6 Variations (Beethoven), p. 238

Composing Project

Create a two-phrase melody (eight measures long) based on the following major chord progression.

Phrase 1:   I | I | V7 | V7 |
Phrase 2:   I | I | V7 | I ‖

First limit yourself to 𝅗𝅥 and ♩ and use only chord tones. When this is completed, add passing tones (p.t.) and neighboring tones (l.n. or u.n.) to make the melody line more interesting. Remember to place the nonchord tones on weak beats or on weak parts of beats. Your accompaniment can include block chords in the I–V$^6_5$ position or be varied to suit the melody. Label your phrases as parallel or contrasting.

Ensemble Playing

Study (from Op. 823)

Piano 1

Carl Czerny (Austria, 1791–1857)

Piano 2

Streets of Laredo*

Piano 1

American Cowboy Song

As I walked out in the streets of La-re-do, As I walked out in La-re-do one day, I

spied a young cowboy all wrapped in white lin-en, All wrapped in the lin-en as cold as the clay.

Piano 2

---

*Piano 1 and 2 may be performed at one piano or separate pianos.

Repertoire

What is the sectional form of Diabelli's piece? Any similar phrases?

Melody

Moderato

Anton Diabelli (Austria, 1781–1858)

Visually analyze "Promenade" for rhythmic features. What is the meter? Notice that this contemporary piece has some new sounds and combinations of sounds. The composer describes the piece as being "freely tonal with chromatic color tones inserted."

Promenade

Herbert Bielawa (United States, b. 1930)

Notice the perfect fifth intervals in the LH and the thirds and fourths in the RH. Block out the interval positions before performing the piece.

Saturday Smile

So casual   Lynn Freeman Olson (United States, 1938–1987)

Reprinted by permission from *Piano for the Developing Musician*, Book I by Martha Hilley and Lynn Freeman Olson. © 1985, West Publishing Co. All Rights Reserved.

Kabalevsky uses the F major, G minor, and G major triads in this piece. Practice the RH triads in block form and with tones one at a time. Practice LH block chords; notice the added F in the G minor and G major triads.

A Little Dance, Op. 39, No. 9

Allegro molto

Dmitri Kabalevsky (Russia, 1904–1987)

Technique Exercises

Exercise 1: Contrary Motion and Arpeggio Practice the following exercise using arpeggios. Keep the wrists flexible and the arms moving in a gentle outward and upward movement. Transpose to other major keys.

Exercise 2: Extension Fingering   This Hanon exercise requires the fingers to expand to the six-finger position (fingers 1 and 2 skip a note between them) and focuses on the stretch between the fifth and the fourth fingers of the LH ascending and the fifth and the fourth fingers of the RH descending. Begin practicing slowly, lifting the fingers high and playing each note with precision. Gradually increase the speed.

The Virtuoso Pianist, No. 1 (simplified version)

Charles Louis Hanon
(France, 1820–1900)

Exercise 3: Broken Chord (Alberti Bass)   Practice the following two studies for facility in using the broken-chord figure in both hands. This particular figure when performed in the bass is often called the **Alberti bass.** (Eighteenth-century composer Domenico Alberti used these figures in his sonatas.)

Part A

Part B

Chapter Evaluation

1. Play the primary chords in the I–IV$_4^6$–V$_5^6$ position in the following major keys with correct fingering: C, G, D, A, E, F, B♭, E♭, A♭.

2. Demonstrate legato pedaling by performing the exercise on p. 150.

3. Harmonize one of the melodies on pp. 154–155 with primary chords.

4. Play with rhythmic accuracy a piece in this chapter that has a compound meter.

5. Construct major-minor seventh chords (dominant seventh chords) on the given roots.

6. Label these major triads and major-minor seventh chords as follows: root position (R), first inversion (1st), second inversion (2nd), or third inversion (3rd).

7. Write the primary chords for the stated key in root position and then in the I–IV$_4^6$–V$_5^6$ position.

8. Harmonize "Melody 3" and "Melody 4" with the appropriate chords. Notate the chords on the staff below the melody. Write the chords in the I–IV$_4^6$–V$_5^6$ position.

Melody 3

Key: _____

Melody 4

Key: _____

9. Write a meter signature in compound duple meter _____,
   compound triple meter _____, and compound quadruple meter
   _____.

10. Create and notate a rhythmic phrase in the specified meters and lengths.
    Use a variety of note possibilities.

❖ Nine

❖ MELODY

The Minor Scales

The major and minor scales are the scale patterns that serve as the basis for most **tonal music.** Major scales have one pattern, whereas **minor scales** *come in three forms: natural minor, harmonic minor, and melodic minor.* Each form has a particular pattern of whole and half steps. All three forms have in common a half step between the second and the third scale degrees.

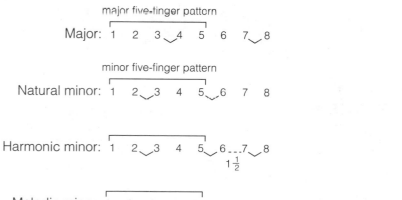

Natural Minor Scale

The **natural minor scale** (probably the oldest form of the minor scale) includes five whole steps and two half steps. The half steps occur between steps 2 and 3 and steps 5 and 6. The natural minor scale pattern is represented by the white keys from A to A.

A natural minor scale

Performing the Natural Minor Scale

1. Practice the A natural minor scale with the tetrachord fingering. Pay close attention to the whole and half steps.

2. Sight-read "Hatikvah" with the tetrachord fingering.

Hatikvah (excerpt)   Israeli National Anthem

3. Perform the following piece, which uses pitches in the D natural minor scale. The RH stays within the minor five-finger pattern.

Melody, Op. 39, No. 3 (from *24 Little Pieces*) Dmitri Kabalevsky (Russia, 1904–1987)

Natural Minor Scale (One-Hand Fingering)

Crossover and crossunder fingering is needed to play the natural minor scale with one hand. The fingering for the A natural minor scale (also the same for E, D, G, and C minor scales) is as follows:

A natural minor scale

Performing the Natural Minor Scale (One-Hand Fingering)

1. Practice the following thumb-under exercise in preparation for one-hand minor scale playing. Keep the hand in position and let the thumb do all the work.

Thumb-Under Exercise in Minor

2. Perform the A natural minor scale with one-hand fingering in two octaves—in contrary motion and in parallel motion.

Minor Key Signatures

Relative Major and Minor Key Signatures

The minor key signatures may be related to major key signatures, for each major key shares a key signature with a minor key. Major and minor scales with the same key signature are referred to as **relative.**

The key signatures and the tonics are the same for natural, harmonic, and melodic minor scales. However, the natural minor is the only form that uses the pitches indicated by the key signature exclusively.

Relative major and minor key signatures

Guidelines for Determining the Tonic or Minor Key

To identify the minor tonic or key, it is easiest to first locate the *major tonic.* Then count down three half steps (or a minor third) to the *minor tonic.* When a major tonic is in a space, the minor one is in the next lower space. When a major tonic is on a line, the minor one is on the next lower line.

The Circle of Fifths

The fifteen minor key signatures progress in a sequence of perfect fifths. This sequence can be arranged in a circle of fifths, as the major keys are. By moving clockwise *up* the interval of a perfect fifth to the tonic, each new key adds one more sharp. By moving counterclockwise *down* a perfect fifth, each new key adds one more flat. The three enharmonic keys appear at the bottom of the circle.

The circle of fifths (minor keys)

Enharmonic Keys

Harmonic Minor Scale

The **harmonic minor scale** is the most frequently used. It is the form upon which chords (harmonies) are usually built. The harmonic minor scale has the same half steps between 2 and 3 and 5 and 6 as the natural minor but raises the seventh degree one half step, creating a step and a half between 6 and 7. (The raised seventh also establishes a half step between 7 and 8, as in the major scale.) The raising of the seventh tone is accomplished by an accidental rather than by a change in the key signature. The key signature is the same for natural minor and harmonic minor.

A harmonic minor scale

Performing the A Harmonic Minor Scale (Tetrachord Fingering)

1. Practice the A harmonic minor scale with the tetrachord fingering. Be conscious of the whole and half steps, and listen for that familiar "pull" from 7 toward 8.

2. Perform "Israeli Folk Melody 3," which uses the A harmonic minor scale. Notice that the G♯ (seventh step) is added in the music.

Israeli Folk Melody 3

3. Perform the following harmonic minor scale tetrachord exercises.

Harmonic Minor Scale Tetrachord Exercise—Sharp Keys Beginning with A minor, build harmonic minor scales at the keyboard using the tetrachord fingering. Follow the LH-over-RH format used in the tetrachord fingering of major scales. For example, place your LH on the upper tetrachord of the A minor scale (E F G♯ A), making this the lower tetrachord of the E harmonic minor scale. Remember to cover the RH notes quickly with the LH.

A harmonic minor   *E harmonic minor*

Harmonic Minor Scale Tetrachord Exercise—Flat Keys Beginning with the A♭ minor scale, build harmonic minor scales using the tetrachord fingering. Follow the same LH-over-RH format.

A♭ harmonic minor   *E♭ harmonic minor*

Harmonic Minor Scale (One-Hand Fingering)

The harmonic minor scales have different one-hand fingerings.* The fingering follows for the A harmonic minor scale (also the same for the E, D, G, and C minor scales).

---

*One-hand fingerings for all minor scales are shown in Appendix E.

A harmonic minor scale

Performing the Harmonic Minor Scale (One-Hand Fingering)

1. Practice the A harmonic minor scale with one-hand fingering in two octaves—first in contrary motion and then in parallel motion.

2. Once the fingering is secure for the A minor scale, try the E, D, G, and C minor scales.

Melodic Minor Scale

Of the three forms of minor, the **melodic minor** is used the least. This scale has the same half steps between 2 and 3 as natural and harmonic but raises both the sixth and the seventh steps one half step. The melodic minor usually descends in the natural minor form. (As with the harmonic form, if the raising of the sixth and seventh steps requires an accidental, this is added in the melody, not in the key signature.)

A melodic minor scale

Melodic Minor Scale (One-Hand Fingering)

The one-hand fingering for the A melodic minor scale follows. This fingering is also the same for the E, D, G, and C melodic minor scales.

A melodic minor scale

Performing the A Melodic Minor Scale

1. Practice the A melodic minor scale, first with the tetrachord fingering and then with the one-hand fingering (two octaves). Listen to the raised sixth and seventh ascending and the return to natural minor in the descending portion.

2. Measures 2 and 3 of "Yesterday" are based on the A melodic minor scale. Notice the raised sixth and seventh in the melody. Play this portion of the song with the RH. (The entire song is on p. 269.)

John Lennon (England, 1940–1980)
Paul McCartney (England, b. 1942)

Yesterday (excerpt)

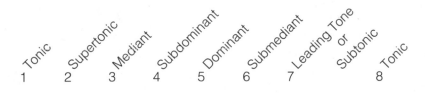

Identification of Scale Tones

Scale Degrees

The degrees of the minor scales are identified by the same names as those of the major scale—with the exception of the seventh in the natural minor form. Since the natural minor scale does not have a half step between the seventh and the eighth degrees, the seventh degree is often referred to as the **subtonic.**

Minor scale degrees

Syllable Names

Pitches in the minor scales may be referred to with syllable names, just as in major. Two approaches are used for associating syllables with pitches in minor keys.

1. Scales begin with *do* as in major, and the remaining syllables are altered when necessary. This approach stresses the relationship of the sound of the tonic with the syllable *do*.

2. Scales begin with *la* and end on *la* (the tonic or keynote is *la*). This approach stresses the relationship between the major and minor scales.

A natural minor scale

| do | re | me | fa | sol | le | te | do |

| la | ti | do | re | mi | fa | sol | la |

A harmonic minor scale

| do | re | me | fa | sol | le | ti | do |

| la | ti | do | re | mi | fa | si | la |

A melodic minor scale

| do | re | me | fa | sol | la | ti | do | te | le | sol | fa | me | re | do |

| la | ti | do | re | mi | fi | si | la | sol | fa | mi | re | do | ti | la |

Identifying Minor Keys

Determine the minor key for each of the following pieces. Follow these guidelines:

1. Examine the key signature to determine the major and minor possibilities.

2. To eliminate one possibility (from guideline 1), check the final pitch of each piece. Most often, that will be the tonic.

3. If you think a minor tonic is indicated, check the melody to see if accidentals are used. Remember the harmonic and melodic minor scales will have accidentals added to the melody.

Adagio

Daniel Gottlob Türk (Germany, 1750–1813)

English Carol

Stairway to Heaven (excerpt)

Jimmy Page (England, b. 1944)
Robert Plant (England, b. 1948)

There's a la - dy who's sure all that glit - ters is gold— and she's

buy - ing a stair - way to heav - en. when she gets there she knows if the

stores all are closed with a word she can get what she came for.

Canon   Konrad Max Künz (Germany, 1812–1875)

❖ **HARMONY**

Primary Chords in Minor

To construct the primary chords in minor,* the harmonic minor scale usually serves as the framework. The i and iv chords are always minor, and the V and V7 chords are always major and major-minor sevenths (as in a major key).

Primary chords in A minor

i, iv$_4^6$, and V$_5^6$ Chords in Selected Minor Keys

As in major, the primary chords in minor can be rearranged or inverted for ease in moving from one chord to the next. The same inversions for the iv (second inversion) and V7 (first inversion) are used in harmonic minor.

Key of A minor

---

*i, iv, and V7 chords for minor keys are shown in Appendix G. RH and LH fingerings are also provided.

Key of E minor

Em	Am	B7
i	iv$^6_4$	V$^6_5$

Key of B minor

Bm	Em	F#7
i	iv$^6_4$	V$^6_5$

Key of D minor

Dm	Gm	A7
i	iv$^6_4$	V$^6_5$

Key of G minor

Gm	Cm	D7
i	iv$^6_4$	V$^6_5$

Key of C minor

Cm   Fm   G7

i   iv$_4^6$ V$_5^6$

Key of F minor

Fm   B♭m   C7

i   iv$_4^6$ V$_5^6$

Performing i–iv$_4^6$–V$_5^6$

1. Perform the following exercise to practice the moves between the three chords. When you move from i to iv$_4^6$, notice how the bottom notes of the two chords stay the same while the middle note moves up a whole step and the top note moves up a half step. When changing from the i to the V$_5^6$, the top note stays the same, the middle note moves up a whole step, and the bottom note moves down a half step. The fingerings and whole-half step moves will be the same in any minor key. Memorize this progression. Learn to shift quickly and smoothly from one chord to another. Feel the shape of the next chord, and actually touch the keys just before playing. Transpose this exercise to other minor keys.

i–iv$_4^6$–V$_5^6$ Exercise

2. Use legato pedaling for the next exercise of the primary chords. Try not to blur chord tones or overlap sounds of single notes. Connect evenly when crossing hands. Transpose to other minor keys.

Arpeggio Exercise: i–iv$^6_4$–V$^6_5$

3. Perform the following pieces. Determine the minor key and the primary chords first; then practice the chord progression. Be sure to review the rhythm, form, and fingering for each piece before performing.

Chording with i and V$^6_5$

Folk Melody 8

Transpose to B minor

Folk Melody 9

Transpose to D minor

Chording with i, iv⁶₄, and V⁶₅

This Old Hammer

American Folk Melody

This old ham-mer___ killed John Hen-ry,___ This old ham-mer___

___ killed John Hen-ry,___ This old ham-mer___ killed John Hen-ry,

___ But it won't kill me,___ But it won't kill me.___

Czechoslovakian Folk Melody 2

5   1   3   5   1   2

Transpose to D minor

Joshua Fought the Battle of Jericho

Moderato

Black American Spiritual

Josh-ua fought the bat-tle of Jer-i-cho,— Jer-i-cho,— Jer-i-cho;—

Josh-ua fought the bat-tle of Jer-i-cho,— And the walls came tum-bling down. You may

talk a-bout your kings of Gid-e-on, You may talk a-bout your men of

Saul, But there's none like good old Josh-ua at the bat-tle of Jer-i-cho.

Harmonizations with i, iv, and V7 Chords

Accompany the following melodies with the i, iv, and V7 chords. (Refer to guidelines on p. 153). Try different accompaniment patterns (broken chord and arpeggio) too.

Chording with i and V⁶₅

Folk Melody 10

Hungarian Folk Melody 2

German Dance No. 1 (excerpt)   Franz Schubert (Austria, 1797–1828)

Chording with i, iv⁶₄, V⁶₅

Canterbury   English Folk Melody

Folk Melody 11

Relative Majors and Minors

Major and minor scales sharing the same key signatures are *related* (see "Minor Key Signatures" earlier in this chapter). Often in compositions, especially long pieces, both the major and the relative minor (or vice versa) are used.

"We Three Kings of Orient Are" is in E minor in the A section and in G relative major in the B section. Practice one section at a time. Notice the $\frac{3}{8}$ time signature:

$$\left(\begin{array}{l} 3 = 3 \text{ beats in a measure} \\ 8 = \text{♪ receives one beat} \end{array} \right)$$

We Three Kings John H. Hopkins (United States, mid 19th c.)

Parallel Majors and Minors

Just as major and minor scales and keys can have the same key signature in common but have different tonics, so major and minor scales and keys can have the same tonic but different key signatures. When a major and minor scale begin on the same tonic, they are said to be *parallel majors and minors*. For example, C major and C minor are **parallel keys.**

C major   *C minor*

"Ah, vous dirai-je, Maman" is presented here in its original scale (C major) and in the parallel minor. Play both versions.

Ah, vous dirai-je, Maman (C major)

Ah, vous dirai-je, Maman (C minor)

❖ **FORM**

Theme and Variations

Since the 1600s, keyboard players have performed compositions based on the form **theme and variations.** A theme and variations is a series of variations on a given melody. Although some theme and variations are improvised at the keyboard, many composers over the years have written a set of variations on a popular song or dance, a chorale tune, or a theme they or someone else composed.

Variations are created by altering the rhythm, melody, or harmony (or all three) of the **theme.** For example, the rhythm could be altered by changing the meter, or the melody could be varied by changing from major to minor or vice versa. If "Ah, vous dirai-je, Maman" were used as the theme for such a composition, one variation could include the change of mode from major to minor (as in the parallel minor example). Another variation could feature a change of meter from $\frac{4}{4}$ to $\frac{3}{4}$.

In 1778 Wolfgang Amadeus Mozart composed a set of variations on the theme "Ah, vous dirai-je, Maman." The theme follows in its entirety, but only excerpts of the twelve variations are included. Study this example and determine the melodic, rhythmic, and harmonic changes made for each variation. A live or recorded performance of Mozart's entire composition will help you to hear what you see and see what you hear.

12 Variations on "Ah, vous dirai-je, Maman," K. 265*

Theme　　　　　　　　　　　　　　　　　Wolfgang Amadeus Mozart (Austria, 1756–1791)

---

*The *K* used in W. Mozart's works is an abbreviation for Köchel. L. von Köchel chronologically catalogued Mozart's more than 600 compositions.

Var. I (excerpt)

Var. II (excerpt)

Var. III (excerpt)

Var. IV (excerpt)

Var. V (excerpt)

Var. VI (excerpt)

Var. VII (excerpt)

Var. VIII (excerpt)

Var. IX (excerpt)

Var. X (excerpt)

Var. XI (excerpt)

Adagio

Var. XII (excerpt)

Allegro

Composing Projects

1. Create your own theme and variations composition. Choose a simple, familiar melody that you can play well. Some ideas are "Lovely Evening," p. 144; Czechoslovakian Folk Melody 1, p. 82; "Kum Ba Yah," p. 155; and

"I Never Will Marry," p. 152. Write at least one variation illustrating a change of mode (major, minor) and one showing a rhythmic change.

2. Compose a keyboard piece in A B A form. Each section should include at least two phrases. Write one of the sections in a contrasting mode (major or minor). Decide on a chord progression for your sections, and then add nonchord tones for variety. Some chord progressions that could be used arc as follows:

Section A: I or i | IV or iv | I or i | V7 |
                 V7 | I or i | V7 | I or i ‖

Section B: I or i | I or i | V7 | I or i |
                 I or i | IV or iv | V7 | I or i ‖

Ensemble Playing

Shalom, Chaverim*

Piano 1   Israeli Round

Piano 2

---

*"Shalom" may also be performed as a round. Piano 2 could play an introduction (last two measures of Piano 2 part), then play throughout and finish with a two-measure coda (same as introduction). Two groups of pianists could perform Piano 1 part. The second group could begin when the first has reached the last beat of measure 1. Repeat as many times as you wish. At one piano, play "Shalom" with Piano 1 part an octave higher and Piano 2 as notated.

"Zum Gali Gali" may be performed by three groups of pianists* as follows:

Piano 1   Perform this ostinato for a two-measure introduction, throughout the piece and as a two-measure coda.

Ostinato

Piano 2   After Piano 1's introduction, play "Zum Gali Gali."

Piano 3   Begin the melody when Piano 2 begins measure 5.

Zum Gali Gali

Israeli Folk Melody

---

*At one piano, Piano 1 can be performed as written while Piano 2 is played an octave higher.

Repertoire

Notice the minor five-finger range for "Round Dance." What can you say about the pitches in the final measure?

Round Dance (from *First Term at the Piano*)

Andante moderato

Béla Bartók (Hungary, 1881–1945)

In this Kabalevsky piece, which interval is used almost exclusively? Notice the jump from the ascending interval to the descending one. First practice measures 1–3 separately very slowly, using the drop/lift technique (see Chapter 7). Then work on the entire piece.

Op. 39, No. 4 (from *24 Little Pieces*)   Dmitri Kabalevsky (Russia, 1904–1987)

What is the overall form of "Minuet"? Notice that the A section is in minor (which form?). The B section begins in relative major F but quickly moves back to D minor.

Minuet   Leopold Mozart (Austria, 1719–1787)

Technique Exercises

Exercise 1: Extension Fingering and Interval Study This exercise focuses on the intervals within the three minor scales. Notice the new intervals: the minor sixth (m6) and the minor seventh (m7). (Remember, minor intervals are always a half step smaller than major ones.) Feel the distance as you play, and listen to the sound of each. Practice hands separately and hands together. Transpose to other minor keys.

Natural minor

Harmonic minor

Melodic minor

Exercise 2: Contraction Fingering   This exercise stresses contraction within the five-finger pattern. Fingers are actually brought closer together. Practice hands separately and hands together. Play without accidentals (in parentheses) for the major pattern and with accidentals for the minor pattern. Transpose to the parallel major and minors of G, F, D, A, E, and B.

Exercise 3: Technical Study   After this study is secure as notated, change to the C parallel minor (harmonic).

Study (from Op. 823)   Carl Czerny (Austria, 1791–1851)

Exercise 4: Independent Use of Fingers In this exercise, the thumb and the little finger play the whole notes, while the other fingers play the quarter notes. Practice hands separately first, then hands together. Change to the parallel minor; then transpose to other major and minor patterns.

Part A

Part B

Chapter Evaluation

1. Play the pitches in the natural, harmonic, and melodic minor scales on the following tonics: D, G, E, and C.

2. Perform the G harmonic minor scale in two octaves ascending and descending.

3. Play the i, iv$_4^6$, V$_5^6$ chords in the following minor keys (harmonic form): A, E, B, D, and G.

4. Demonstrate parallel majors and minors by choosing a major melody to play. Perform the melody in major and in the parallel minor.

5. Perform the following melody accurately and musically. Be able to describe the melodic and rhythmic characteristics and its overall design. Transpose the melody to the key of D minor. Harmonize with i and V7 chords.

Bim Bom

Israeli Folk Melody

6. The three forms of minor scales are _____ ,

_____ , and _____ .

7. Write the specified minor scales.

D harmonic   *C natural*   *G harmonic*

A melodic   *E harmonic*

8. Identify the minor tonics for the following key signatures.

(a)   (b)   (c)   (d)   (e)   (f)

(g)   (h)   (i)   (j)

9. Write the primary chords for the stated key in root position and then in the
i–iv$^6_4$–V$^6_5$ position.

E minor

i   iv   V7   i   i   iv$^6_4$ V$^6_5$ i

G minor

i   iv   V7   i   i   iv$^6_4$ V$^6_5$ i

10. Describe the theme and variations form.

Ten

❖ MELODY

Pentatonic Scales

Although major and minor scales have been widely used in the music of Western civilization and are certainly the most familiar to us, other scales and modes have been used and are still being used today. Of all the scales, the **pentatonic scale** (*penta* means five) may be the oldest. This five-tone scale serves as the basis for much of world music, particularly music of Northeast Asia, Native America, Africa, and Europe, and it often forms the basis of ostinati in rock music. Pentatonic melodies are also found in the works of Western art music composers, for example, Debussy's "Voiles."

The pentatonic scale most frequently used includes no half steps and one interval of a whole step plus a half step. This familiar pentatonic scale can be illustrated on the five black keys.

This pentatonic scale can be transposed to the white keys of the piano.

Major and minor key signatures are adapted for pentatonic music by choosing the signature that results in the five necessary pitches. The key signature will not always identify the tonic as it does for major and minor scales. Because there is no leading tone in the pentatonic scale, some pentatonic music does not have an obvious tonic.

Performing Pentatonic Melodies

1. Play the preceding pentatonic scale on the black keys, and then transpose to the white keys.

2. Perform "Taiwan School Song" as written, then on the black keys by thinking of each note as being sharped.

Taiwan School Song

© 1981, Patricia Hackett. Used by permission. (*The Melody Book*, 2nd ed. Englewood Cliffs, N.J.: Prentice-Hall, Inc., 1991.)

3. Perform "Sakura," which uses a pentatonic scale that includes half steps (E F A B C). Notice the drone accompaniment.

Sakura

Japanese Folk Melody

4. Perform other pentatonic melodies in *PianoLab*:

   "Tom Dooley," p. 147
   "Amazing Grace," p. 263
   "Kang Ding City," p. 253
   "Auld Lang Syne," p. 257

5. Improvise with the pentatonic scale by playing only on black keys. Review "Playing the Black Keys" and "Improvisation in the Boogie-Woogie Style," in Chapter 1.

Modes

Modes (seven-tone scales) served as the basis of most Western music through the seventeenth century. Between 1700 and 1900 the modes, from which our major and minor scales emerged, were seldom used. However, nineteenth- and twentieth-century composers rediscovered modal scales. Modes are used today in classical music, jazz, and popular music. Often, contemporary composers mix modes and scales within a piece.

Basically, the modes, also referred to as *church modes*, are seven-tone scales that include five whole steps and two half steps. Together with major and minor scales, they can be illustrated on the white keys of the piano.

As with minor scales, two approaches are used for associating syllables with modes.

1. The mode begins with *do.* The remaining syllables are altered when necessary.

2. The keynote is *do.* Each mode begins with the syllable name that pitch would have in the major scale of that key. This approach stresses the relationship of the modes to the tonic of the major scale (Dorian is up a major second, Phrygian is up a major third, and so on).

Major scale

RH   1   2   3   1   2   3   4   5

LH   5   4   3   2   1   3   2   1

do   re   mi   fa   sol   la   ti   do

Dorian mode (natural minor with raised 6th)

RH   1   2   3   1   2   3   4   5

LH   5   4   3   2   1   3   2   1

do   re   me   fa   sol   la   te   do
re   mi   fa   sol   la   ti   do   re

Phrygian mode (natural minor with lowered 2nd)

RH   1   2   3   1   2   3   4   5

LH   5   4   3   2   1   3   2   1

do   ra   me   fa   sol   le   te   do
mi   fa   sol   la   ti   do   re   mi

Lydian mode (major with raised 4th)

RH   1   2   3   1   2   3   4   5

LH   5   4   3   2   1   3   2   1

do   re   mi   fi   sol   la   ti   do
fa   sol   la   ti   do   re   mi   fa

Mixolydian mode (major with lowered 7th)

RH   1   2   3   1   2   3   4   5

LH   5   4   3   2   1   3   2   1

do   re   mi   fa   sol   la   te   do
sol   la   ti   do   re   mi   fa   sol

Minor scale (natural)

RH   1   2   3   1   2   3   4   5

LH   5   4   3   2   1   3   2   1

do   re   me   fa   sol   le   te   do

Locrian mode (seldom used)

The modes may be transposed to any pitch, but because of the variety of whole-half step formulas, they may be more difficult to recognize in transposed form. Often major and minor key signatures are adapted for transposed modal music. The Dorian and Mixolydian modes are especially popular with composers of jazz and commercial music. (Much of the Beatles' music is modal, frequently mixing modes and major and minor within a piece.)

Performing the Modes

1. Practice each of the preceding modes, listening for the special qualities of each. The fingering is indicated above and below the notes.

2. Choose a mode and improvise a bit at the keyboard with the pitches in that mode. Move freely between left and right hands. Experiment until you come up with something that pleases you.

3. Perform the following two pieces. Determine which mode each is based on (both are in original form, not transposed form).

Scarborough Fair

English Folk Song

The Great Silke

Scottish Folk Melody

The Whole-Tone Scale

Scales using equidistant tones are common in Southeast Asia and enjoyed a brief vogue in early twentieth-century Europe, especially in the music of the French Impressionist composers Debussy and Ravel. The **whole-tone scale,** a six-tone scale, consists solely of whole steps. The two forms of the whole-tone scale are shown here.

As used by the Impressionist composers, this scale lacks a feeling of tonic and conveys ambiguity, a sense of vagueness, a musically indefinite quality (an impression). Since no major or minor key signature can be used for whole-tone music, accidentals are included in the music.

Performing Whole-Tone Scales

1. Improvise on the whole-tone scale with the damper pedal depressed. Freely move between the low, middle, and high registers of the piano. Use arpeggio figures. Be experimental with rhythms.

2. Analyze "Wholes," noting the use of both forms of the whole-tone scale, the compound meter, and what happens between the LH and the RH in the second part of the composition. The ⁹ marks mean to lift for a brief "breath" or pause. Perform as much as you can of this challenging piece.

Wholes

Cantabile (♩. = 120)   Herbert Bielawa (United States, b. 1930)

© 1982, Herbert Bielawa. Used by permission.

3. Rebikov's "The Bear," on p. 228, is another challenging composition that uses the whole-tone scale.

The Blues Scale

The special form of jazz called the blues uses a **blues scale.** This scale can only be approximated in traditional notation or on the keyboard because the "blue notes" fall somewhere between the pitches and keys we know. To approximate the pitches in a blues scale, take the traditional major scale and flat the third and the seventh pitches (the fifth is also flatted in some of the music of the bebop era).

Blues scale

Performing the Blues Scale

1. Play the blues scale in C (as in the preceding example) hands separately. Experiment with rhythmic variations as you get familiar with the sound of the scale. Transpose the blues scale to F major and to G major.

2. Perform "Scaling the Blues." Notice how the C, the F, and the G blues scales are all included.

Scaling the Blues

3. Review the ensemble piece "Razzle Dazzle" by Lee Evans in Chapter 7. This piece is based on the blues scale.

Bitonality

Twentieth-century composers have explored the use of two or more **tonalities** (or keys) occurring simultaneously. When two tonalities are performed at the same time, the result is **bitonality.**

Performing Bitonal Music

1. Perform Bartók's "Dialogue," which may be considered bitonal. The RH part is within the A minor five-finger pattern, and the LH part is within the E major pattern. Practice the parts separately and together.

Dialogue (from *First Term at the Piano*)   Béla Bartók (Hungary, 1881–1945)

Moderato

2. Improvise with bitonality. Use a different major or minor five-finger pattern in each hand. Be flexible with rhythm. Explore various registers of the piano and the use of pedal.

Atonality

Twentieth-century composers have also experimented with pitch organizations that suggest no tonality or key. Music in which all pitches have an equal function and no one tone serves as the tonic is referred to as **atonal.**

Tone Rows

One atonal pitch organization involves arranging the twelve pitches of the chromatic scale (a twelve-tone scale consisting entirely of half steps) into a series (**serial music**), or a **twelve-tone row.** Thousands of rows can be formed from the chromatic scale. The series is then used without alteration according to the following rules.

1. O—**Original:** Row is played exactly in the planned order, one note after the other.

O

2. R—**Retrograde:** Row is played backwards, one note after the other.

3. I—**Inversion:** Row is played with the same intervals of the original, but with each interval inverted (upside down or in "mirror" version).

4. RI—**Retrograde Inversion:** Row is played in inverted form in retrograde (backwards and upside down).

R-I

Performing Tone Rows

1. Perform the original form of the tone row in any rhythm you choose or without any rhythm at all. Use both hands to play each note in any register you wish. Follow this rule: Once you have used a tone in the row, do not reuse it until the other eleven tones have been used.
2. Perform all four forms of the tone row.
3. Discover which forms of the preceding tone row are used in "Two-Handed Duet." Remember that any octave position and enharmonic spelling of the pitches are possible, and any clef, range, simultaneous playing of tones, and repetition of tones may be used. Notice how the rhythm ties the composition together.

Two-Handed Duet (X from *32 Piano Games*)

♩ = 160

Ross Lee Finney (United States, b. 1906)

❖ RHYTHM

Shifting Meter

A rhythmic effect of irregularity can be achieved by **shifting meters.** Shifting meter occurs when there are meter changes throughout a composition—for example, $\frac{3}{4}$ to $\frac{4}{4}$ to $\frac{3}{4}$. To indicate shifting meters, a new meter signature is written within each measure where the meter changes.

Rhythm Exercise: Shifting Meter   Clap, count, or play on any key(s) the following examples of shifting meters.

5. [rhythm exercise]

6. [rhythm exercise]

7. [rhythm exercise]

8. [rhythm exercise]

9. [rhythm exercise]

10. [rhythm exercise]

Performing Shifting Meter

Stravinsky's "Andantino" shifts from $\frac{2}{4}$ to $\frac{3}{4}$ to $\frac{2}{4}$ at the end of the first section. Clap and count the rhythm before playing. Notice that both hands stay within the five-finger position; note the A B A form of the piece.

Andantino (No. 1 from *The Five Fingers*)   Igor Stravinsky (Russia, 1882–1971)

Asymmetric Meter

Asymmetric meter occurs when the accents within a measure are spaced irregularly. This gives an effect of constant shifting of accents throughout an entire piece and is often heard in Eastern European and Greek music and in twentieth-century music.

Asymmetric meters

Performing Asymmetric Meters

1. Perform "Yugoslavian Folk Melody" in 7/8, observing that the accents occur on beats one and five. Clap the rhythm of the RH part before playing.

Yugoslavian Folk Melody

2. Clap the rhythm of this excerpt from Dave Brubeck's "Blue Rondo a la Turk." In the first three measures, the accents occur on beats one, three, five, and seven of the 9/8 meter, and in the last measure, the accents occur on beats one, four, and seven. Perform when the rhythm is secure.

Blue Rondo a la Turk (excerpt)

Dave Brubeck (United States, b. 1920)

3. "Clusterphobia" includes shifting meter ($\frac{5}{4}$ to $\frac{3}{4}$), asymmetric meter ($\frac{5}{4}$), and no meter (0). The five-note clusters are to be performed entirely on white keys with fingers 1-2-3-4-5 in both hands. Both damper and soft pedals remain down throughout.

Clusterphobia

Very slowly

Nancy Van de Vate (United States, b. 1930)

Free tempo

Composing Projects

1. Create a two-phrase melody based on D Dorian (white keys D to D) or G Mixolydian (white keys G to G). Organize the pitches so that the tonic or tonal center is established and the melody concludes on the tonal center. Because the half step between 6 and 7 gives the Dorian mode its characteristic sound, include these pitches if your melody is in Dorian. If your melody is in Mixolydian, feature the whole step between 7 and 8, and conclude with a move up from 7 to 8.

2. Compose a whole-tone piece. First, choose the whole-tone scale and create a piece based on these pitches with dynamic and tempo variations. Use the different registers of the piano. Experiment with pedaling to give a blurred, indefinite quality to your composition.

3. Create a twelve-tone row composition. First, establish your tone row, arranging the twelve pitches of the chromatic scale in a way that sounds satisfying to you. Add rhythm to the row. Distribute the row between the LH and the RH and notate. Manipulate the row in original and retrograde forms as many times as you wish to complete the piece. Consider dynamics, tempo, and shifting meters.

Ensemble Playing

Every Night When the Sun Goes In*

Piano 1

American Folk Song

© 1962 by James Leisy Music. Used by permission.

---

*Play Piano 1 an octave higher and Piano 2 as notated for one piano and two pianists.

Piano 2

Some say "Every Night When the Sun Goes In" is based on the Mixolydian mode (note the flatted seventh), and others say it is based on a blues scale.

Jazzmatazz

Piano 1 (Students)

Cheerfully, with a bounce (♩ = 92)   Lee Evans (United States, b. 1933)

_____
loco = play in the octave written.

Piano 2 (Teacher)

Cheerfully, with a bounce (♩ = 92)

Repertoire

"Joy" stays within the D to A range in both hands. Notice the two measures that include chromatic tones with the RH. As you practice hands together, observe the **imitation** between lines. What is the form of this piece?

Joy

Allegretto   Cornelius Gurlitt (Germany, 1820–1901)

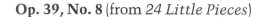

Visually analyze Op. 39, No. 8 for key or mode identification, phrase structure, interval movement, fingerings, and rhythm. Play legato, paying careful attention to slurs.

Op. 39, No. 8 (from *24 Little Pieces*)

Andante   Dmitri Kabalevsky (Russia, 1904–1987)

The interval of a major sixth (nine half steps) is featured in this **etude.** Only fingers 1 and 5 are used. Practice the major sixths alone first, then the entire piece.

Etude No. 9

Very fast (♩ = 112)   John Biggs (United States, b. 1932)

© 1981 John Biggs. Reprinted from *12 Little Etudes* (Consort Press, 1717 N. State College, Fullerton, CA 92631). Used by permission.

Leopold Mozart's "Minuet" is an example of A B, or binary, form. Notice how each section is repeated, and discover what part of A is repeated in B. Practice one section at a time.

Minuet

From *Nannerl Notenbuch* (1759)
Leopold Mozart (Austria, 1719–1787)

This minuet is one of the keyboard pieces included in the music book compiled by Leopold Mozart for his eight-year-old daughter, Nannerl. As a child, Nannerl concertized throughout Europe with her younger brother, Wolfgang Mozart, and won praise for her extraordinary keyboard skills.

Technique Exercises

Exercise 1: Extension Fingering   This exercise extends beyond the five-finger range and works on the third, fourth, and fifth fingers of the LH ascending and the third, fourth, and fifth fingers of the RH descending. At first, practice very slowly, lifting fingers high and playing each note distinctly and evenly (hands together and then hands separately). Gradually increase the speed. Play legato.

The Virtuoso Pianist, No. 4
(simplified version)

Charles Louis Hanon (France, 1820–1900)

Exercise 2: Changing Fingers Practice this exercise with each hand separately. Change fingers while holding down the half notes. Also play the exercise changing between the following fingers:

RH: 3–2, 4–3, 5–4

LH: 2–3, 3–4, 4–5

Part A

Part B

Exercise 3: Independent Use of Fingers   In this exercise, the thumb and the
little finger sustain notes, while the other fingers move independently. Practice
with each hand alone and then hands together. Transpose to other major and
minor patterns.

Part A

Part B

Exercise 4: Legato or Syncopated Pedaling   Practice this Schumann piece
slowly, using the legato or syncopated pedaling. Practice hands separately and
then hands together.

Ein Choral
(from *Piano Pieces for the Young*, Op. 68)   Robert Schumann (Germany, 1810–1856)

Chapter Evaluation

1. At the keyboard, demonstrate a pentatonic scale, the Dorian mode, the
   Mixolydian mode, and a whole-tone scale.
2. Demonstrate changing fingers on the same key by playing Technique Exercise 2 in this chapter.

3. Play the bitonal piece "Dialogue" (Bartók), p. 208, with pitch and rhythmic accuracy. Be able to identify the two keys used.

4. Perform the twelve-tone row composition "Two-Handed Duet," p. 210, with pitch and rhythmic accuracy. Be prepared to discuss the tone row and its manipulation in this piece.

5. Clap several examples of shifting meter in the rhythm exercise in this chapter.

6. Demonstrate legato pedaling by performing Schumann's "Ein Choral" (Technique Exercise 4).

7. Write the pitches in the pentatonic scale based on the following whole-half step arrangement.

   A ___ ___ ___ ___
      W   W   W&H   W

8. Notate the pitches in the designated modes on the staff and on the keyboard chart.

Dorian

Mixolydian

9. The following excerpt from a Chopin mazurka uses the pitches Bb C D E F G A Bb. Determine on which mode this excerpt is based.

_____
      (mode)

Mazurka in F Major, Op. 68, No. 3 (excerpt)

Poco più vivo

Frédéric Chopin (Poland, 1810–1849)

10. Write whole-tone scales on the given pitches.

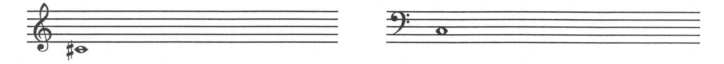

11. In music, when two tonalities or keys are heard simultaneously, the result
is known as _____.

12. Create a twelve-tone row and notate the row on the following staff.

13. One way to manipulate a tone row is to play it backwards or in
_____ form.

14. Notate four measures of a rhythm in any asymmetric meter of your choice.

Supplementary Music

Supplementary Classical Piano Literature

What is the finger pattern for the LH and the RH in this piece? Observe the RH rests and staccato markings. Is the LH part similar to a particular accompaniment pattern?

Folk Song (No. 7 from *First Term at the Piano*)

Moderato

Béla Bartók (Hungary, 1881–1945)

"Little Rondo" includes only an A and a B section. Work on the A section of this **rondo** (the LH part is a good technical exercise). What is different about measures 9–16? When the A section is secure, continue to the B.

Little Rondo

Daniel Gottlob Türk (Germany, 1750–1813)

Determine the key and the primary chords for this **bagatelle**. For section B, write the roman numeral identification for the chords in each measure.

Bagatelle

Moderato   Anton Diabelli (Austria, 1781–1858)

Minuets and other short pieces written in the eighteenth century are in two-part form (A B). Mozart's "Minuet in G" is a good example of binary form. Notice how easy it is to divide the melody into two-measure and four-measure groupings. How many measures are in each section? Practice one section at a time.

Minuet in G, K. 1

Wolfgang Amadeus Mozart (Austria, 1756–1791)

A child prodigy, Mozart wrote this minuet in 1761 or 1762 in Salzburg, Austria. The trio, a part of this minuet, is omitted in the preceding example.

---

* ♩♩♩ is a triplet (three notes of equal value within a beat that normally divides into two's: ♩♩).

Identify the scale for Vladimir Rebikov's composition. What accompaniment figure is used in the LH?

The Bear

Andante   Vladimir Rebikov (Russia, 1886–1920)

Perform this eighteenth-century minuet in a moderate tempo and in the normal touch (*non legato*) of the period.

Minuet

From *Notenbuch für Wolfgang* (1762)
Carl Philipp Emanuel Bach (Germany, 1714–1788)

"Schwaebisch" (rustic dance) follows the eighteenth-century two-part form. Break down each section into smaller parts. How many measures seem to group together?

Schwaebisch

Johann Christoph Friedrich Bach
(Germany, 1732–1795)

Since "Growing" has no meter signature, what can you determine about the
meter?　Which note gets the beat?

Growing

Moderately slow　　　　　　　　　　　　　　　　　　　　Emma Lou Diemer (United States, b. 1927)

What is the sectional form for Rameau's "Minuet"?

Minuet

Allegretto

Jean Philippe Rameau (France, 1683–1764)

Identify the key in which "March" begins and ends. What happens in the middle section?

March (from *Six Children's Pieces*)

Tempo di marcia   Dmitri Shostakovich (Russia, 1906–1975)

Notice the parallel motion between hands in the opening measures of the Haydn composition. What is the same in the A and B sections?

German Dance, No. 2

Franz Joseph Haydn (Austria, 1732–1809)

Statement (from *Little Piano Book*, Op. 60)

Allegro (il ritmo sempre molto preciso)   Vincent Persichetti (United States, 1915–1987)

Decide whether "Bourrée" is in the major mode or the minor mode. Notice the short upbeat, one of the characteristics of a **bourrée.**

Bourrée

From *Notenbuch für Wolfgang* (1762)
Leopold Mozart (Austria, 1719–1787)

This excerpt from the popular "Für Elise" is in A minor. In what section is there a momentary shift to the relative major? Notice the importance of the arpeggio figure in this piece.

Für Elise (excerpt)

Poco moto

Ludwig van Beethoven (Germany, 1770–1827)

What is the sectional form for this minuet? Identify the rhythmic motive
that is used.

Minuet in F, K. 2

Wolfgang Amadeus Mozart (Austria, 1756–1791)

Note the clef used for both the RH and the LH parts in Op. 39, No. 5. Pay
close attention to the staccato and accent marks. Play slowly at first (hands together); then gradually increase your speed.

Op. 39, No. 5 (from *24 Little Pieces*)

Lively

Dmitri Kabalevsky (Russia, 1904–1987)

Consider eighteenth-century performance practices before playing this piece. The touch would most likely be *non legato*; the tempo, *moderato*; and the dynamic level, *mezzo forte*.

Minuet in G

From *Notenbüchlein für Anna Magdalena Bach* (1725)
Johann Sebastian Bach (Germany, 1685–1750)

Notice the compound meter, the LH accompaniment figure, and the grace notes (𝄾). Although the grace notes are to be performed quickly, they do not receive any specific time value.

Theme from 6 Variations on "Nel cor più non mi sento"

Andantino   Ludwig van Beethoven (Germany, 1770–1827)

Piano variations were very popular with composers of the **Classic period.** Beethoven wrote over twenty separate sets of piano variations on original or borrowed themes. "Nel cor più non mi sento" ("Why Feels My Heart So Dormant?") is a borrowed theme from an aria by Giovanni Paisiello.

What is the form for this contemporary piece? Which keys or modes predominate? Observe the tempo, dynamic, and articulation markings.

Pastorale

♩. = 88

Herbert Bielawa (United States, b. 1930)

© 1963, Herbert Bielawa. Used by permission.

Make the melody line "sing." Pay careful attention to phrasing. Notice that the LH part is notated in the treble clef and uses the same accompaniment figure throughout.

Stückchen (from *Piano Pieces for the Young*, Op. 68)

Nicht schnell   Robert Schumann (Germany, 1810–1856)

Does the A section end on the I or on the V? What about the B section? Notice the imitation at times between the RH and the LH. Consider eighteenth-century performance practices in regard to touch, dynamics, and tempo.

Minuet

Wilhelm Friedemann Bach (Germany, 1710–1784)

The Bartók composition, instead of being built on the all-white-key Dorian (D to D), is transposed to A. Before performing the piece, study the phrase structure to see where repeats occur.

III (from *For Children*)

Andante

Béla Bartók (Hungary, 1881–1945)

What kind of triads are used in both hands for the first and last four measures of "Prologue"? Pay close attention to the dynamic and tempo markings throughout the piece.

Prologue (from *Little Piano Book*, Op. 60)

Adagio pesante

Vincent Persichetti (United States, 1915–1987)

The sectional form for this mazurka is _____ _____ _____ . At the end of section B, notice the rolled chords (chord tones quickly "rolled" from bottom note to top; ⦃ = rolled chord).

Mazurka No. 3 (from *24 Mazurkas*)   Maria Szymanowska (Poland, 1789–1831)

Note the shifting meters in "Shifting Shadows." How many sections does
the composition divide into? Are there any similarities between sections?

Shifting Shadows

Slowly (♪ = 108–116)

Nancy Van de Vate (United States, b. 1930)

Slightly faster (♩ = 63)

Prelude, Op. 28, No. 4

Largo

Frédéric Chopin (Poland, 1810–1849)

Supplementary Blues, Boogie, and Ragtime

Analyze the first eight bars of "No Name Blues" and decide if the harmonies are predominantly triads or seventh chords. What rhythmic effect is achieved by eighth rests on the first beats of measures?

No Name Blues

Theresa McGlone

© 1980, Theresa McGlone. Used by permission.

Theresa McGlone composed this piece while enrolled in a beginning piano and music fundamentals course at San Francisco State University.

Notice the rhythmic variety created by the triplet in this blues piece. Why is the grace note important?

Blue, Blue, Blue

Matt Zlatunich

Matt Zlatunich composed this blues composition while a student in a beginning piano and music fundamentals class at San Francisco State University.

The seventh chord (major-minor seventh) is featured throughout this "boogie." Circle and label the nonchord tones in the LH part.

Walkin' Boogie

8va bassa sempre

Another LH pattern for "Walkin' Boogie":

etc.

The Entertainer (A Ragtime Two-Step)
(Sections A and B simplified)

Not too fast   Scott Joplin (United States, 1868–1917)

"The Entertainer" of 1902 played an important role in the ragtime revival of the 1970s when the rag, **ragtime,** and Joplin himself were popularized by the hit movie *The Sting*. Notice the syncopated melody line (accents on offbeats) in "The Entertainer." Practice the characteristic jump bass (stride bass)* in the LH. Refer to the chord sheet in Appendix I for explanation of chord symbols used in this rag.

---

*See Appendix H, 8a and 8b for other stride bass patterns.

Create a jump bass accompaniment (easy stride or full stride) for "Red Rambler Rag." Refer to the patterns in Appendix H, 8a or 8b, and the notated accompaniment in "The Entertainer."

Red Rambler Rag

Julia Lee Niebergall (United States, 1886–1968)

Supplementary Songs with Accompaniments

He's Got the Whole World in His Hands

Black American Spiritual

He's got the whole world in his hands, He's got the whole world in his hands, He's got the whole world in his hands, He's got the whole world in his hands.

Kang Ding City

Chinese Folk Song

Pau ma Iyou, Iyou de shan shang, Yi dwo Iyou, Iyou de yun, Ah! Dwan, dwan Iyou, Iyou de jau dzai,

Kang Ding Iyou, Iyou de cheng, Ah! Ywe lyang, wan, wan, Kang Ding Iyou, Iyou de cheng, Ah!

Silent Night

Joseph Mohr (Austria, 1792–1848)
Franz Gruber (Austria, 1789–1863)

With a Little Help from My Friends
(excerpt—rhythmically simplified)

John Lennon (England, 1940–1980)
Paul McCartney (England, b. 1942)

Sinkiang Folk Dance

Chinese Folk Dance

© 1981, Patricia Hackett. Used by permission. (*The Melody Book*, 2nd ed. Englewood Cliffs, N.J.: Prentice-Hall, 1991.)

Hymne (excerpt)

Slowly   Vangelis Papathanassiau (Greece, 20th c.)

Auld Lang Syne

Scottish Folk Song

Give My Regards to Broadway

George M. Cohan (United States, 1878–1942)

We Shall Overcome

American Freedom Melody

Katherine Lee Bates (United States, 1859–1929)
Samuel A. Ward (United States, 1847–1903)
Arranged by Alexander Post

America, the Beautiful

Memory from *Cats*
(excerpt—rhythmically simplified)

Trevor Nunn, after T. S. Eliot
Andrew Lloyd Webber (England, b. 1948)

Supplementary Songs (Melodies Only)

The following melodies do not have LH accompaniments notated. Rather, suggested chords (by letter name symbols) appear above each melody. These symbols should serve as a guide for creating your own accompaniments. Refer to Appendix I for explanations of unfamiliar chord symbols.

Since the symbols indicate only the letter name and the chord quality, you may choose to use the root of the chord alone, any chord tone, the entire chord in root position, or the chord in one of the inversions studied earlier. You might also choose the accompaniment style in which to perform the chords. Appendix H has numerous accompaniment patterns to try.

Hey Lidee

Saturday Night

Amazing Grace

John Newton (United States, 1725–1807)
Early American Melody

Joy to the World

Isaac Watts
George F. Handel (Germany, 1685–1759)

St. James Infirmary

American Folk Song

Worried Man Blues

American Folk Song

John B.

Caribbean Folk Song

Lucy in the Sky with Diamonds

John Lennon (England, 1940–1980)
Paul McCartney (England, b. 1942)

De Colores

Traditional Mexican Song
Arranged by Joan Baez

Aura Lee

American Folk Song

As the black-bird in the spring, 'Neath the wil-low tree,____

Sat and piped, I heard him sing, Sing-ing Au-ra Lee.

Chorus

Au - ra Lee, Au - ra Lee, Maid of gol-den hair,

Sun-shine came a - long with thee, And swal-lows in the air.

This song was made into the popular song "Love Me Tender" (Elvis Presley).

Michelle

John Lennon (England, 1940–1980)
Paul McCartney (England, b. 1942)

Mi - chelle, ma belle, these are words that go to-geth -er well, my Mi - chelle,

Mi - chelle, ma belle, sont les mots qui vont très bien en-semble, très bien en-semble. I

love you, I love you, I love you. That's all I want to say. Un - til I find a
need you, I need you, I need you. I need to make you see. Oh, what you mean to
want you, I want you, I want you. I think you know by now. I'll get to you some-

way.____ I will say the on - ly words I know that you'll un - der - stand:
me.____ Un - til I do, I'm hop - ing you will know what I
how.____ Un - til I do, I'm tell - ing you so you'll un - der -

2. B *D. S. al coda*
mean. I

Coda
stand, my Mi - chelle.

John Lennon (England, 1940–1980)
Paul McCartney (England, b. 1942)

Yesterday

Yes - ter - day, all my troub - les seemed so far a - way,
Sud - den - ly, I'm not half the man I used to be,

Now it looks as if they're here to stay;_ Oh! I be - lieve_ in yes - ter - day._
There's a shad - ow hang - ing o - ver me;_ Oh! Yes - ter - day__ came sud - den - ly!__

Why she had to go I don't know, she would - n't say.

I said some - thing wrong, now I long for yes - ter - day._____

Yes - ter - day, love was such an eas - y game to play.

Now I need a place to hide a - way;_ Oh! I be - lieve_ in yes - ter - day._

Ensemble Music

Recreation I*

Piano 2 (Teacher)

Andante

Arnoldo Sartorio (Germany, 1853–?)

270

Piano 1 (Students)

Andante

---
*To perform Piano 1 with two students at a piano, one student plays the part as written while the second student plays the part two octaves lower.

Recreation II

Piano 2 (Teacher)

Andante cantabile

Arnoldo Sartorio (Germany, 1853–?)

Piano 1 (Students)

Andante cantabile

Love Somebody

Piano 1

American Folk Song

Piano 2

J'ai du bon Tabac

Piano 1

French Folk Song

Piano 2

Duet Exercise 32*

Piano 2 (Teacher)

Andante   Ferdinand Beyer (1803–1863)

*To perform with two students at one piano, one student plays Piano 1 as written while another plays Piano 1 two octaves lower.

Piano 1 (Students)

Andante

It's Natural to Have a Flat

Piano 1 (Students)

Easy swing

Lee Evans (United States, b. 1933)

Piano 2 (Teacher)

Easy swing

Duet Exercise 42*

Piano 1 (Students)

Andante

Ferdinand Beyer (1803–1863)

Piano 2 (Teacher)

Andante

---

*To perform with two students at one piano, one student plays Piano 1 as written while another plays Piano 1 two octaves lower.

The "Middle Eastern Folk Melody" may be performed by two pianists or two groups of pianists* as follows:

Piano 1   Perform this ostinato for a two-measure introduction, throughout the piece, and as a two-measure coda (ending).

Ostinato

Piano 2   Play the "Middle Eastern Folk Melody" beginning after Piano 1's two-measure introduction.

Middle Eastern Folk Melody

---

*Two pianists seated at one piano could perform Piano 1 and 2 parts with one performer on the Piano 1 part (an octave lower than written) and the other on Piano 2 (an octave higher than written).

St. Paul's Steeple

American Folk Melody

Etude, Op. 82, No. 10

Piano 1

Cornelius Gurlitt (Germany, 1820–1901)

Etude, Op. 82, No. 11

Piano 2

Cornelius Gurlitt (Germany, 1820–1901)

"Come, Follow" may be performed as a round with three groups of pianists.

Come, Follow

John Hilton (England, 1599–1657)
arr. Linda Mankin

Lively

Hello! Ma' Baby

Joseph E. Howard (United States, 1878–1961)
Ida Emerson (United States, late 19th–20th c.)

Piano 1

Piano 2

Razzle Dazzle

Piano 2 (Teacher)

Moderate swing

Lee Evans (United States, b. 1933)

Piano 1 (Students)

Moderate swing

Lovely Evening*

Traditional Round

Transpose to F major

French Canadian Round†

---

*Perform as a round with several groups of pianos. Piano 1 begins the melody. Piano 2 enters when Piano 1 begins measure 7 (2). Piano 3 begins the melody when Piano 2 has reached measure 7. Repeat as many times as desired. (At one piano, one pianist can play Piano 1 part an octave higher while another plays Piano 2 part an octave lower.)

†Perform "French Canadian Round" with two groups of pianists. Piano 1 begins. Piano 2 enters when Piano 1 has reached measure 3. Repeat as many times as desired. (At one piano, a pianist can perform Piano 1 part an octave higher while another performs Piano 2 an octave lower.)

Study (from Op. 823)

Piano 1

Carl Czerny (Austria, 1791–1857)

Piano 2

Streets of Laredo*

Piano 1

American Cowboy Song

Piano 2

---

*Piano 1 and 2 may be performed at one piano or separate pianos.

Shalom, Chaverim*

Piano 1

Israeli Round

Piano 2

*"Shalom" may also be performed as a round. Piano 2 could play an introduction (last two measures of Piano 2 part), then play throughout and finish with a two-measure coda (same as introduction). Two groups of pianists could perform Piano 1 part. The second group could begin when the first has reached the last beat of measure 1. Repeat as many times as you wish. At one piano, play "Shalom" with Piano 1 part an octave higher and Piano 2 as notated.

"Zum Gali Gali" may be performed by three groups of pianists* as follows:

Piano 1   Perform this ostinato for a two-measure introduction, throughout the piece and as a two-measure coda.

Ostinato

Piano 2   After Piano 1's introduction, play "Zum Gali Gali."
Piano 3   Begin the melody when Piano 2 begins measure 5.

Zum Gali Gali

Israeli Folk Melody

Zum ga - li, ga - li, ga - li, Zum ga - li, ga - li, Zum ga - li, ga - li, ga - li, Zum ga - li, ga - li,

He - cha lutz le 'man a - vo - dah, A - vo - dah le 'man - he - cha - lutz.

---

*At one piano, Piano 1 can be performed as written while Piano 2 is played an octave higher.

Every Night When the Sun Goes In*

Piano 1

American Folk Song

Ev-'ry night —— when the sun goes in, —— Ev-'ry night —— when the sun goes in, —— Ev-'ry

night —— when the sun goes in, —— I hang my head —— and mourn-ful cry. ——

Piano 2

8va bassa sempre

(8va bassa sempre)

(8va bassa sempre)

© 1962 by James Leisy Music. Used by permission.

*Play Piano 1 an octave higher and Piano 2 as notated for one piano and two pianists.

Jazzmatazz

Piano 2 (Teacher)

Cheerfully, with a bounce (♩ = 92)   Lee Evans (United States, b. 1933)

Piano 1 (Students)

Cheerfully, with a bounce (♩ = 92)

loco = play in the octave written.

Musical Terms and Signs

Dynamic Terms and Signs

pp Pianissimo: very soft

p Piano: soft

mp Mezzo piano: medium soft

mf Mezzo forte: medium loud

f Forte: loud

ff Fortissimo: very loud

Crescendo (cresc.): gradually louder

Decrescendo (decresc.): gradually softer

Diminuendo (dim., dimin.): gradually softer

Common Tempo Terms

Largo: very slow

Lento: very slow

Adagio: slowly, leisurely

Larghetto: slow

Andante: moderately

Andantino: slightly faster than andante

Moderato: moderately

Allegretto: moderately fast

Allegro: fast, lively

Vivace: animated, lively

Presto: very rapidly

A tempo: return to original tempo

Accelerando (accel.): gradually increasing tempo

Rallentando (rall.): gradually becoming slower

Ritardando (rit.): gradually slower and slower

Ritenuto (riten.): immediately slowing in tempo

Additional Terms and Signs

Accent (>)

Affettuoso: with affection, warmth

Animato, animé: animated; with spirit

Assai: very

Calmado: calmly, tranquil

Cantabile: in singing style

Coda: a concluding section added to the end of a composition

Commodo: conveniently, quietly, easily

Con: with

Con anima: with animation

Con moto: with motion

Con spirito: with spirit

D.C. (Da capo): repeat from the beginning

D.C. al coda (Da capo al coda): return to the beginning and play to the measure marked with coda sign (⊕), concluding with coda

D.C. al fine (Da capo al fine): return to the beginning and conclude with the measure marked *fine*

D.S. (Dal segno): repeat from the sign ⸝

D.S. al coda (Dal segno al coda): return to the sign ⸝ and conclude with the coda

D.S. al fine (Dal segno al fine): return to the sign ⸝ and conclude with the measure marked *fine*

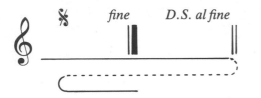

Dolce: sweetly, softly

Espressivo: with expression

Fermata (⌒): hold or pause

Fine: the end

Giocoso: playfully, humorously

Grazioso: gracefully

Legato: smoothly, connected

Leggiero: light, delicate

Loco: place; play as written

Lunga: prolonged pause

Ma non troppo: but not too much

Maestoso: majestically

Marcia: in the style of a march

Meno: less

Molto: much

Mosso: agitated

Moto: motion; speed; movement

Nicht schnell: not fast

Ottava alta (8va⁻ ⁻ ⌐): play an octave higher than written

Ottava bassa (8va⌐ ⌐⌐): play an octave lower than written

Pastorale: simple, tender, flowing

Per: for, by, from, in

Pesante: heavily

Più: more

Poco: little

Preciso: precise

Rinforzando (rf., rfz.): pronounced accent or stress

Risoluto: resolute, bold

Ritmo: rhythm

Rubato: flexibility of tempo with slight ritards for musical expression

Scherzando: playful

Sempre: always, continually

Sforzando (sf., sfz.): a strong accent

Simile: in a similar manner

Sostenuto: sustained

Spirito: spirit, life

Staccato (♪): short, detached

Subito: suddenly, at once

Tenuto (♩): sustain for full value

Tranquillo: calm, quiet

Très expressif: very expressive

Tutti: all (singular: tutto)

Un: one

Valse: waltz

Vivo: lively, spiritedly, briskly

Slur:

Tie:

(play with a down-up motion of the wrist)

(First and Second Endings)

♩ = 80   Tempos are often indicated in *metronome markings*. This example indicates that a metronome (a mechanical device ticking at a desired speed) should be set at 80. The ♩ will be equal to 80 beats or ticks per minute on a metronome.

Treble and Bass Clef Notation

Circle of Fifths (Major and Minor Keys)

Enharmonic Keys

Major Scales (with Piano Fingerings)

Major Scale Degrees

Number	Name
1	*Tonic*
2	*Supertonic* (one whole step above the tonic)
3	*Mediant* (between 1 and 5 and a third above the tonic)
4	*Subdominant* (a fifth below the tonic)
5	*Dominant* (a fifth above the tonic)
6	*Submediant* (a third below the tonic)
7	*Leading tone* (a half step below the tonic)

F# major

C# major

F major

Bb major

Eb major

Ab major

Db major

Gb major

Cb major

Selected Minor Scales (with Piano Fingerings)

Minor Scale Degrees

Number	Name
1	*Tonic*
2	*Supertonic* (one whole step above the tonic)
3	*Mediant* (a third above the tonic)
4	*Subdominant* (a fifth below the tonic)
5	*Dominant* (a fifth above the tonic)
6	*Submediant* (a third below the tonic)
7	*Leading tone* (a half step below the tonic)
	or
	Subtonic (a whole step below the tonic)

Intervals and Chords

Intervals

An *interval* is the pitch distance between two tones. Intervals are identified by the number of steps they encompass and by quality. The five qualities are as follows: perfect (P), major (M), minor (m), diminished (d or °), and augmented (A or +).

	P1	m2	M2	A2	m3	M3	d4	P4	A4
Half steps:	0	1	2	3	3	4	4	5	6

	d5	P5	A5	m6	M6	A6	d7	m7	M7	P8
	6	7	8	8	9	10	9	10	11	12

Triads

The four kinds of triads (three-note chords) are *major, minor, augmented,* and *diminished.*

Major   *Minor*   *Augmented*   *Diminished*

Triads in major scale†   *Triads in harmonic minor scale*

Major	Minor	Minor	Major	Major	Minor	Dim.	Minor	Dim.	Aug.	Minor	Major	Major	Dim.
C: I	ii	iii	IV	V	vi	vii°	a: i	ii°	III+	iv	V	VI	vii°

---

*bb (**double flat**). A double flat lowers a pitch one whole step.

†Chords built on steps 1, 4, and 5 of a major or minor scale are primary chords. Chords built on steps 2, 3, 6, and 7 are **secondary chords.**

Seventh Chords

The seventh chord consists of four notes: a triad with an added seventh. There are five types of seventh chords: *major-minor*, *major-major*, *minor-minor*, *diminished-minor*, and *diminished-diminished*. Each seventh chord also has a common name, shown in the following chart. Use the terms recommended by your instructor. See also Appendix I.

Seventh Chord Type	Symbols	Common Name
Major-minor seventh	7 or Mm7	Dominant seventh
Major-major seventh	maj7 or MM7	Major seventh
Minor-minor seventh	m7 or mm7	Minor seventh
Diminished-minor seventh	half-dim7 or ∅7	Half-diminished seventh
Diminished-diminished seventh	dim7 or dd7 or ∅7	Diminished seventh

Major-minor (dominant) seventh chord

Major-major seventh chord

Minor-minor seventh chord

Half-diminished seventh chord

Diminished seventh chord

❖ Appendix G

Selected Primary Chords

A harmonic minor

i   iv   V7   i   i   iv⁶₄   V⁶₅   i

E harmonic minor

i   iv   V7   i   i   iv⁶₄   V⁶₅   i

B harmonic minor

i   iv   V7   i   i   iv⁶₄   V⁶₅   i

F♯ harmonic minor

i   iv   V7   i   i   iv⁶₄   V⁶₅   i

C♯ harmonic minor

i   iv   V7   i   i   iv⁶₄   V⁶₅   i

D harmonic minor

i   iv   V7   i   i   iv⁶₄   V⁶₅   i

G harmonic minor

i   iv   V7   i   i   iv⁶₄   V⁶₅   i

C harmonic minor

i   iv   V7   i   i   iv⁶₄   V⁶₅   i

F harmonic minor

i   iv   V7   i   i   iv⁶₄   V⁶₅   i

Accompaniment Patterns

8b. Jump bass (full stride)   or

9. Boogie bass

10. Boogie-woogie walking bass

11. Boogie-woogie barrel-house bass

12. Rocking bass

13. Rock bass

14. Funk-rock bass

15. Blues bass

16. Western bass

17. Walking bass

18. Rock rhythm

19. Rock ostinato

20. Habañera

Chords and Chord Symbols (Lead Sheet Notation)

Key for Chord Symbols

1. A capital letter indicates a major triad.
2. A capital letter followed by a lowercase *m* indicates a minor triad.
3. A capital letter followed by *dim* or a small circle (○) indicates a diminished triad.
4. A capital letter followed by *aug* or a plus sign (+) indicates an augmented triad.
5. When any of the preceding letters and symbols are followed by the numeral 7, a seventh chord is indicated. (See also Appendix F.)
6. When any of the preceding letters and symbols are followed by a 6, a major sixth is added above the root.

*×(**double sharp**). A double sharp raises a pitch one whole step.

Chords over Bass Notes

In jazz and popular music, chords are often superimposed over a bass note. In such cases, two capital letters, separated by a slash (/), are used—for example, C/G or Cm7/F. The first symbol indicates the chord to be played and the second symbol specifies the bass notes.

Electronic Keyboards

Electronic keyboards may be grouped into three categories: *basic keyboards, digital pianos,* and *synthesizers.*

Basic Keyboards

Basic keyboards are the most commonly purchased (and the least costly) non-professional electronic keyboards. Their most attractive features, outside of price, are battery operation, portability, and self-contained speaker systems. In addition, all basic keyboards include preprogrammed rhythmic accompaniments and automatic chordal accompaniments.

Preprogrammed Rhythmic Accompaniments

Basic keyboards typically offer approximately ten to twenty preprogrammed rhythm patterns (percussion only—no pitched sounds). For example, one preprogrammed rhythmic accompaniment might be an eight-beat pattern of one to two measures of eighth notes in $\frac{4}{4}$. This pattern could be used as a rhythmic accompaniment for a rock, soul, or pop song. Most preprogrammed accompaniments feature a drum set and a variety of percussion instruments. Although the choices are labeled, some experimentation is often necessary to find the correct rhythmic accompaniment for a particular song.

Virtually all keyboards allow the player to vary the tempo of the selected rhythm. A player should experiment with tempo and rhythmic combinations to make the appropriate accompaniment choice.

Automatic and Fingered Chordal Accompaniments

Most basic keyboards offer a split keyboard (one that is divided into two or more sections), with the lower one and one-half octaves serving as the on-demand automatic accompaniment section. When the automatic accompaniment function is activated, a chordal accompaniment and a bass line are added to the selected rhythm in the proper style and tempo.

In the "fingered" or manual mode, the player must play (and finger) all the notes in the chord. Again, the style and tempo of the actual chordal accompaniment depends on the selected rhythm.

Manual or Fingered Mode

Fingered—C chord   *Actual sound (8-beat rhythm pattern)*

The "one-touch" mode allows the player to *depress only the chord root* to sound a major triad accompaniment (once the selected rhythm is activated).

"One-Touch" Mode

Fingered—C chord   *Sound (no rhythm)*

Other chords may be sounded by depressing additional keys. The systems made by Casio and Yamaha, the two major manufacturers of electronic keyboards, differ in the selection of additional keys to sound the various chords. In the Casio system, the root of the chord is always the lowest note fingered and a major triad is automatically sounded. By depressing any combination of one, two, or three *higher* pitches (*as long as they are within the accompaniment section of the split keyboard*), the player may sound the minor triad, major-minor seventh chord, and minor seventh chord variations.

Casio System

Fingered—Cm chord   *Sound*

Fingered—C7 chord   *Sound*

Fingered—Cm7 chord   *Sound*

In the Yamaha system, *any* white key added that is *lower* than the root will change the major triad to a major-minor seventh chord (dominant seventh chord); *any* black key *lower* than the root will change it to a minor triad.

Yamaha System

Fingered—G7 chord   *Sound*

Fingered—Gm chord   *Sound*

Performance Suggestions for Fingered and Touch Modes

1. In both fingered and "one-touch" modes, there is no need to hold down a key (or keys) to repeat a chordal accompaniment *as long as the selected rhythm is activated.*

2. Some songs may be accompanied with a rhythmic pattern, and others may sound better without a preprogrammed rhythmic accompaniment. Therefore, two styles of LH playing are necessary.

   a. When using rhythmic accompaniments in both the fingered and the "one-touch" modes, it is not necessary or advisable to hold down a key(s) to repeat a chordal accompaniment.

   b. When the rhythmic function is not used, the keys must be depressed continuously by the player. (Some timbre choices on the keyboard will naturally include more sustain than others—for example, violin and organ.) Once again, experimentation is important.

3. In the fingered mode, the player may use chord inversions without altering the root in the bass. This is an effective feature that makes LH chording much easier for the beginning and the intermediate player.

It takes considerable practice and patience to learn the individual idiosyncrasies of an electronic keyboard. However, portable basic keyboards offer many features that can develop one's musical understandings, as well as features that make playing more fun and interesting.

Digital Pianos

Unlike basic keyboards and synthesizers, digital pianos are distinguishable because they have the look and, more important, the feel (weighted action) of a conventional acoustic piano. One of the important differences is a digital piano's MIDI (Musical Instrument Digital Interface) capabilities. This capability allows it to be used as a controller keyboard for other MIDI instruments, allows a performer to "record" a melody and then "play" it back at the touch of a button (called *sequencing*), and offers choices of preprogrammed timbres. The timbre choices might include the distinctive sounds of specific brands of pianos, organ sounds, or string sounds. Some even offer the capability to make the instrument sound as though it is being played in a room, on a stage, or in a large concert hall. Performance techniques for digital pianos, when employing an acoustic piano sound, are the same as for any acoustic piano.

Synthesizers

Synthesizers, the most electronically sophisticated of the three groups of instruments, offer far more options in terms of programmability than either basic keyboards or digital pianos. They also come in many styles, types, and sizes.

Generally, synthesizers do not include preprogrammed rhythmic accompaniments, self-contained speaker systems, or automatic chording. Some do specialize in sampling (a digital "recording" of any acoustic sound), and others include on-board sequencers, as opposed to a separate electronic sequencing device like a computer. Performance techniques for synthesizers are quite different from those used for acoustic and digital pianos, mostly because of the lighter, organlike action. Ultimately, instrument or timbre selection will dictate performance techniques.

Selected Bibliography

Anderton, Craig. *Midi for Musicians.* New York: Amsco Publications, 1986.

Crombie, David. *The New Complete Synthesizer.* London: Omnibus Press, 1986.

Hurtig, Brent, ed. *Synthesizers and Computers.* Rev. ed. Cupertino, Calif.: GPI Publications, 1987.

Velton, Geary. *The Rock Synthesizer Manual.* Woodstock, Ga.: Rock Tech Publications, 1986.

Timeline of Western Art Music and History

Musical Style Periods	Medieval ca. 500–ca. 1420	Renaissance ca. 1420–ca. 1600	Baroque ca. 1600–ca. 1750
Music Elements	*Melody:* moves mostly in steps; limited vocal range; uses church modes *Harmony:* monophonic; polyphonic for 2 to 4 voices; use of imitation in 14th c. *Rhythm:* moves in free chant rhythm; beat groupings of 3s in 13th c.; beat groupings of 2s in 14th c. *Form:* free vocal chant forms; songs with verses, hymns; free and fixed poetic forms for secular music *Timbre:* small choirs (monophonic chants); soloists (polyphonic music); instrumental music (generally improvised)	*Melody:* moves mostly in steps; expanded vocal range *Harmony:* 4 parts; use of imitation; dissonance (cadence points); text painting *Rhythm:* beat groupings of 2s; syncopation; more complex rhythms *Form:* fixed poetic forms are replaced by imitation; songs with verses; hymns *Timbre:* polyphonic; 5 or more voices in 16th c.; homophony; music for specific instruments; secular: soloists, small ensembles; sacred: small choirs, polyphony	*Melody:* moves in steps and skips; sequential; use of ornamentation *Harmony:* major-minor scales; polyphonic; homophonic; chord progressions I–IV–V *Rhythm:* free (recitative); steady, clear meters *Form:* A B and A B A; fugue; development of multimovement compositions *Timbre:* small choral groups; small orchestras—strings, winds, continuo; soloists
Types of Compositions	mass; plainchant setting of parts of the mass; motet (mostly secular); secular songs; instrumental dances	polyphonic settings of parts of mass; motet; secular songs; instrumental dances; instrumental pieces	mass and motet with instrumental accompaniment; opera; cantata; oratorio; sonata; concerto; fugue; suite
Musical and Historical Events and Figures	Benedictine Order founded (ca. 530) First Crusade (1096–1099) Alhambra Palace (1238–1358) Marco Polo travels to China (1271) Dante (1265–1321) Chaucer (ca. 1340–1400)	Invention of printing press (ca. 1440) Beginning of music printing (ca. 1500) Leonardo da Vinci (1452–1519) Michelangelo (1475–1564) Columbus discovers America (1492) The Reformation (1517) Shakespeare (1564–1616)	First Black slaves to U.S.A. (1619) Harvard University (1636) First public opera house (Venice, 1637) Isaac Newton (1642–1727) Reign of Louis XIV (1643–1715) Reign of Peter the Great (1682–1725) Early pianoforte (1709)

Classic ca. 1750–ca. 1820	Romantic ca. 1820–ca. 1900	Contemporary ca. 1900–
Melody: motivic; short phrases, 8-bar phrases	*Melody:* lyrical; phrases less regular; longer phrases	*Melody:* tone rows
Harmony: major-minor scales; use of modulation; change of key within a movement; homophony	*Harmony:* major-minor scales; expanded use of modulation and chromaticism; harmony; counterpoint	*Harmony:* major-minor scales; atonal; new methods of tonal harmony; homophony; counterpoint; polytonality
Rhythm: free (recitative), clear meters; rhythmic variety	*Rhythm:* variety of meters; varied rhythmic patterns; meter change within movements	*Rhythm:* variety of meters; varied rhythmic patterns; shifting meter, asymmetric meter
Form: sonata; rondo; theme and variations; A B and A B A; multimovement compositions	*Form:* multimovement works; classical forms are expanded	*Form:* forms of all previous periods are used, with extensive changes; freer forms developed
Timbre: instruments more prominent than voice; larger orchestra—without use of continuo	*Timbre:* growth of orchestra; large chorus; large bands; small ensembles	*Timbre:* same as previous periods; large bands; emphasis on percussive sound
mass; oratorio, opera; solo concerto; unaccompanied sonata; instrumental works: symphony, concerto, sonata, string quartet	classical forms are expanded; symphonic poem; solo song cycle; piano character piece	forms from all previous periods are used and expanded; impressionism; expressionism; electronic music; minimalism
Benjamin Franklin (1706–1790)	Darwin (1809–1882)	Airplane invented (1903)
George Washington (1732–1799)	Dickens (1812–1870)	World War I (1914–1918)
Goethe (1749–1832)	Marx (1818–1883)	Russian Revolution (1917)
Development of string quartet (ca. 1750)	Victoria (1819–1901)	First recordings of jazz (1917)
Industrial Revolution (ca. 1770)	Freud (1856–1939)	Television (1929)
American Declaration of Independence (1776)	Invention of phonograph (1877)	Martin Luther King, Jr. (1929–1968)
French Revolution (1789)	Einstein (1879–1955)	World War II (1939–1945)
		Invention of long-playing records (1948)
		Development of indeterminate music (1950s)
		Beatles come to U.S.A. (1963)
		Moon walk (1969)

Timeline of Selected Keyboard Composers and Keyboard Instruments

Musical Style Periods and Composers	Medieval ca. 500–ca. 1420	Renaissance ca. 1420–ca. 1600	Baroque ca. 1600–ca. 1750
	Landini (1325–1397)	Tallis (ca. 1505–1585)	Schütz (1585–1672)
	Paumann (ca. 1410–1473)	Cabezón (1510–1566)	Scheidt (1587–1654)
		A. Gabrieli (ca. 1533–1585)	Hilton (1599–1657)
		C. Merulo (1533–1604)	Froberger (1616–1667)
		Morley (1557–1602)	Lully (1632–1687)
		Bull (1562–1628)	Buxtehude (1637–1707)
		Sweelinck (1562–1621)	Pachelbel (1653–1706)
		O. Gibbons (1583–1625)	de La Guerre (1659–1729)
			Purcell (ca. 1659–1695)
			Couperin (1668–1733)
			Telemann (1681–1767)
			Rameau (1683–1764)
			Handel (1685–1759)
			J. S. Bach (1685–1750)
			D. Scarlatti (1685–1757)
			----------(Pre-Classic)----------
			W. F. Bach (1710–1784)
			C.P.E. Bach (1714–1788)
			L. Mozart (1719–1787)
			J.C.F. Bach (1732–1795)
			Kirnberger (1721–1783)

The Development of Keyboard Instruments	Organ (portative/positive)		Simplified church organ (pipe)
		Fretted clavichord	Unfretted clavichord
		Harpsichord	
		Virginal	

Classic ca. 1750–ca. 1820	Romantic ca. 1820–ca. 1900	Contemporary ca. 1900–
Haydn (1732–1809)	Schubert (1797–1828)	Debussy (1862–1918)
Martines (1744–1812)	L. Farrenc (1804–1875)	Satie (1866–1925)
Türk (1750–1813)	Fanny Mendelssohn Hensel (1805–1847)	Beach (1867–1944)
		Joplin (1868–1917)
Clementi (1752–1832)	Felix Mendelssohn (1809–1847)	Scriabin (1872–1915)
W. A. Mozart (1756–1791)	Chopin (1810–1849)	Rachmaninoff (1873–1943)
Müller (1767–1817)	R. Schumann (1810–1856)	Schoenberg (1874–1951)
---	Liszt (1811–1886)	Ravel (1875–1937)
Beethoven (1770–1827)	Kunz (1812–1875)	de Falla (1876–1946)
Diabelli (1781–1858)	C. Schumann (1819–1896)	Bloch (1880–1959)
Kuhlau (1786–1832)	Köhler (1820–1886)	Bartók (1881–1945)
M. Szymanowska (1789–1831)	Hanon (1820–1900)	Stravinsky (1882–1971)
Czerny (1791–1857)	Gurlitt (1820–1901)	Webern (1883–1945)
	Franck (1822–1890)	"Jellyroll" Morton (1885–1941)
	Gottschalk (1829–1869)	Niebergall (1886–1968)
	Brahms (1833–1897)	Prokofiev (1891–1953)
	Saint-Saëns (1835–1921)	Milhaud (1892–1974)
	Mussorgsky (1839–1881)	Cowell (1897–1965)
	Tchaikovsky (1840–1893)	Gershwin (1898–1937)
	Grieg (1843–1907)	Copland (b. 1900)
	Sartorio (1853–?)	Kabalevsky (1904–1987)
	---	"Fats" Waller (1904–1943)
	Janáček (1854–1928)	Shostakovich (1906–1975)
	MacDowell (1860–1908)	Finney (b. 1906)
	Rebikov (1866–1920)	Cage (b. 1912)
	K. Szymanowski (1882–1937)	Persichetti (1915–1987)
		Monk (1918–1982)
		Diemer (b. 1927)
		Musgrave (b. 1928)
		Bielawa (b. 1930)
		Van de Vate (b. 1930)
		Reich (b. 1936)
		Glass (b. 1937)
		Olson (1938–1987)
		T. Johnson (b. 1939)
		Hays (b. 1941)
		Jarrett (b. 1945)

Electronic (rotary-powered organ)

Pianoforte   Upright piano   Electronic piano

Celesta

Synthesizer   Electronic keyboards

Digital piano

Biographical Sketches of PianoLab Composers

Bach, Carl Philipp Emanuel (Germany, 1714–1788): Brilliant keyboard performer at the court of Frederick the Great; son of J. S. Bach; composed keyboard works, orchestral works, and concertos; author of the important treatise *Essay on the True Art of Playing Keyboard Instruments* (1753).

Bach, Johann Christoph Friedrich (Germany, 1732–1795): Composer and court chamber musician at Bückeburg, Germany; son of J. S. Bach; composed chamber and keyboard music, keyboard concertos, cantatas, and oratorios.

Bach, Johann Sebastian (Germany, 1685–1750): Outstanding composer of the late Baroque period; wrote cantatas, passions, and other choral works; organ, harpsichord, and clavichord works; chamber and orchestral music; harmonized hundreds of chorales.

Bach, Wilhelm Friedemann (Germany, 1710–1784): Composer and keyboardist; eldest son of J. S. Bach; wrote numerous keyboard, instrumental, and choral works.

Bartók, Béla (Hungary, 1881–1945): Composer of string quartets, orchestral works, operas, and piano-teaching pieces; instrumental in collecting Hungarian folk music and incorporating it into his works.

Beethoven, Ludwig van (Germany, 1770–1827): Outstanding composer of the late eighteenth and early nineteenth centuries; his music represents the culmination of the Classic period and an important beginning to the Romantic period; composed nine symphonies, seventeen string quartets, thirty-two piano sonatas, an opera, piano concertos, and chamber music.

Bielawa, Herbert (United States, b. 1930): Composer and professor of theory and composition at San Francisco State University; compositions include electronic works, chamber music, keyboard works (solo and ensemble), and a variety of vocal and instrumental pieces.

Biggs, John (United States, b. 1932): Southern California composer; chosen as composer-in-residence for six colleges in northeastern Kansas from 1967 to 1971; performs in his own John Biggs Consort throughout the world.

Brahms, Johannes (Germany, 1833–1897): Late Romantic period composer and pianist; master of the "variation" compositional device; wrote four symphonies, concertos, chamber music, choral works, songs, and keyboard pieces.

Brubeck, Dave (United States, b. 1920): One of the most notable musicians of the jazz era; his legendary quartet, the most popular combo of the fifties, was one of the first to issue live recordings of concerts.

Chopin, Frédéric (Poland, 1810–1849): One of the foremost keyboard composers of the early Romantic period; wrote many mazurkas, études, preludes, ballades, waltzes, polonaises, and fantasies, and two piano concertos.

Cohan, George M. (United States, 1878–1942): Composer, actor, producer, and playwright; wrote many musical comedies and popular songs, frequently with patriotic themes.

Czerny, Carl (Austria, 1791–1857): Pianist and pedagogue who composed symphonies, overtures, chamber music, and masses and other sacred music; known for his numerous collections of piano studies and exercises.

Denver, John (United States, b. 1943): Singer, composer, guitarist, environmentalist; received international recognition as composer of Peter, Paul, and Mary's hit "Leavin' on a Jet Plane"; other number one hits included "Sunshine on My Shoulders" and "Annie's Song."

Diabelli, Anton (Austria, 1781–1858): Viennese publisher and composer; composed a waltz theme on which Beethoven based his "Diabelli Variations."

Diemer, Emma Lou (United States, b. 1927): Professor of theory and composition at the University of California, Santa Barbara; compositions include works for orchestra and band, chamber ensemble, organ, piano, and chorus as well as solo songs and song cycles.

Emerson, Ida (United States, late 19th–20th c.): Composer who collaborated on several songs with lyricist Joseph Howard.

Evans, Lee (United States, b. 1937): Pianist, composer, performer, and teacher; specializes in teaching a "classical" approach to jazz.

Farrenc, Louise (France, 1804–1875): Pianist, composer, professor of piano at Paris Conservatoire (only woman musician in the nineteenth century to hold a permanent position of this rank and importance); editor of early music.

Finney, Ross Lee (United States, b. 1906): Composer of songs, piano and organ pieces, chamber music, choral works with orchestra, concertos, four symphonies, and other orchestral works.

Gurlitt, Cornelius (Germany, 1820–1901): Keyboardist, composer, and teacher who wrote operas, orchestral and choral works, chamber music, song cycles, and numerous piano pieces.

Handel, George Frideric (Germany, 1685–1759): Composer who, with J. S. Bach, represents the culmination of the late Baroque period; works include many operas, oratorios (for example, *Messiah*), concertos, and chamber music.

Hanon, Charles Louis (France, 1820–1900): Writer of a collection of sixty technique exercises (*The Virtuoso Pianist*) that has become one of the standard technical keyboard works.

Haydn, Franz Joseph (Austria, 1732–1809): Oldest of the three leading composers of the Classic period (with Mozart and Beethoven); wrote 104 symphonies and 88 string quartets, as well as oratorios, choral music, operas, and keyboard music.

Hays, Doris (United States, b. 1941): Pianist, composer, and recording artist who is known for her recordings of the piano music of Henry Cowell and other "cluster" composers; compositions include electronic works, sound sculptures, and mixed media works, as well as more conventional forms.

Hilton, John (England, 1599–1657): Composer and organist; wrote *Catch That Catch Can* (1652), a collection of catches, rounds, and canons.

Howard, Joseph E. (United States, 1878–1961): Composer-singer of early Broadway musicals who wrote the lyrics for several songs with composer Ida Emerson, one of which was the popular "Hello Ma' Baby."

Johnson, Tom (United States, b. 1939): Contemporary composer, pianist, writer, and music critic; much of his music, which reflects a "minimalist" attitude, explores visual and verbal, as well as musical, media.

Joplin, Scott (United States, 1868–1917): Composer and pianist known as the "King of Classic Ragtime"; in addition to his fifty or more piano pieces, he wrote songs, a ragtime ballet, and two operas.

Kabalevsky, Dmitri (Russia, 1904–1987): Composer who wrote operas, ballets, symphonies, incidental music for plays and films, as well as numerous piano pieces; in addition to composing, he became an important spokesperson on Soviet cultural policy, a teacher, and an administrator.

Köhler, Louis (Germany, 1820–1886): Composer of operas, orchestral and vocal works, and numerous piano studies; he also published a number of theoretical and pedagogical writings.

Kristofferson, Kris (United States, b. 1936): Vocalist, composer, guitarist, and actor whose country superstar image is a result of his classic songs "Me and Bobby McGee," "Help Me Make It Through the Night," "Sunday Morning Coming Down," and "For the Good Times."

Lennon, John (England, 1940–1980): Composer, vocalist, guitarist, and founding member of the number one recording group of all time, the Beatles; the Lennon/McCartney (fellow Beatle Paul McCartney) songwriting duo was one of popular music's most successful collaborations.

McCartney, Paul (England, b. 1942): Composer, vocalist, guitarist, bassist with legendary Beatles; collaborated with fellow Beatle John Lennon on most of the band's most popular songs.

Manone, Joseph ("Wingy") (United States, b. 1904): Swing-era jazz trumpeter, with one arm; also a singer and bandleader; his "Tar Paper Stomp" became the hit "In the Mood" for Glenn Miller's band.

Martines, Marianne (Austria, 1744–1812): Vocalist, pianist, teacher, and composer; wrote oratorios, motets, psalms, symphonies, piano concertos, cantatas, masses, and keyboard sonatas; founded her own singing school, which she operated out of her home.

Morrison, Jim (United States, 1943–1971): Composer, vocalist, poet, and leader of the Doors, the Los Angeles–based rock group that he helped form in 1965; hit singles include "Light My Fire" and "Riders on the Storm."

Mozart, Leopold (Austria, 1719–1787): Composer, pianist, and father of Wolfgang Amadeus Mozart; wrote operas, oratorios, cantatas, masses and other sacred choral works, symphonies, concertos, and chamber music; compiled music books of keyboard pieces for his son and daughter, Nannerl.

Mozart, Wolfgang Amadeus (Austria, 1756–1791): With Haydn and Beethoven, one of the finest composers of the Viennese Classic period; a child prodigy, Mozart wrote a vast quantity of music, including keyboard pieces, operas, symphonies, concertos, chamber music, and choral music.

Müller, August Eberhard (Germany, 1787–1817): Conductor, flautist, keyboard player, pedagogue, and composer of concertos, keyboard and chamber music, and various vocal works.

Niebergall, Julia Lee (United States, 1886–1968): Pianist and ragtime composer who is known as one of the leaders in the development of Indianapolis ragtime; composed three rags.

Olson, Lynn Freeman (United States, 1938–1987): Composer, author of many piano books, and music educator; his work has appeared on several highly successful children's television shows.

Persichetti, Vincent (United States, 1915–1987): Composer of nine symphonies, orchestral works, concertos, an oratorio, choral and band works, chamber music, piano and organ pieces, and numerous songs; author of *Twentieth-Century Harmony*.

Rameau, Jean Philippe (France, 1683–1764): Composer, theorist, and organist; wrote numerous operas, chamber cantatas, canons, motets, and keyboard music.

Rebikov, Vladimir (Russia, 1866–1920): Composer whose early works were in the Romantic style, but about 1900 began writing expressionist dramatic and vocal pieces using whole-tone harmony and other contemporary idioms.

Sartorio, Arnoldo (Germany, 1853–?): Author of a piano method book and composer of numerous instructive piano pieces.

Scarlatti, Domenico (Italy, 1685–1757): Composer and harpsichordist who wrote hundreds of compositions for the harpsichord and is credited with innovations that led to the modern keyboard style.

Schubert, Franz (Austria, 1797–1828): One of the leading composers of early romanticism, his works include over six hundred songs, eight symphonies, piano works, chamber music, and music for the stage.

Schumann, Robert (Germany, 1810–1856): One of the most important of the many pianist-composers of the nineteenth century; wrote numerous songs and short piano pieces in addition to symphonies, concertos, and chamber music.

Shostakovich, Dmitri (Russia, 1906–1975): One of the leading symphonic composers of the twentieth century; wrote symphonies, operas, chamber music, and keyboard works.

Stravinsky, Igor (Russia, 1882–1971): An original and sometimes revolutionary composer of the twentieth century; wrote influential scores for ballets, orchestral works, and operas, and explored a wide variety of styles, including jazz and ragtime.

Szymanowska, Maria (Poland, 1789–1831): Acclaimed as one of the greatest women pianists of the nineteenth century and one of the first women composers of Poland; composed mainly piano character pieces: études, nocturnes, and mazurkas.

Türk, Daniel Gottlob (Germany, 1750–1813): Composer, violinist, organist, and teacher of the Classic period (Mozart and Haydn were his contemporaries); known for his keyboard pieces and the method book *Klavierschule*.

Valens, Ritchie (Richard Valenzuela; United States, 1941–1959): Guitarist, singer, songwriter; first Mexican-American Rock performer; his first hit single was "La Bamba" (sung in Spanish) and was based on the Spanish folk song of the same name.

Van de Vate, Nancy (United States, b. 1930): Composer of orchestral, chamber, vocal, and keyboard works; her music has been performed in eighteen countries on four continents; founder of the International League of Women Composers.

Vangelis (Vangelis Papathanassiau, Greece, 20th c.): Composer and keyboard player who first gained recognition as leader of the group Aphrodite's Child; won an Oscar for best score for the Oscar-winning movie *Chariots of Fire*.

Webber, Andrew Lloyd (England, b. 1948): Composer of the scores of numerous hit musicals and popular operas, notably *Cats* and *Phantom of the Opera*.

Glossary

A B   A musical design consisting of two sections, A and B, that contrast with each other (binary).

A B A   A musical design consisting of three sections, A B A. Two are the same and the middle one is different (ternary).

accent   A stress or emphasis given to certain tones. An accent sign is >.

accidental   A sign introduced before a note of a composition that changes the pitch for one measure only: ♯ (sharp), ♭ (flat), ♮ (natural).

accompaniment   Music that goes with or provides harmonic or rhythmic support for another musical part (usually a melody).

Alberti bass   A left-hand accompaniment (named after the eighteenth-century keyboard composer, Domenico Alberti) consisting of a figure of broken chords.

alla breve (¢)   A term indicating two beats to a measure (duple meter); usually stands for $\frac{2}{2}$.

anacrusis (ana-CREW-sis)   An unaccented beat, often the last beat of a measure.

arpeggio, arpeggiated   A pattern in which every tone of the chord is played separately, one after the other.

asymmetric meter   Meter in which the beat groupings are irregular, as $\frac{5}{4}$ or $\frac{7}{8}$. Often created by combining two meters: $\frac{2}{4}$ and $\frac{3}{4} = \frac{5}{4}$.

atonal   Twentieth century music in which no tonic or key center is apparent.

augmented triad   A three-note chord built with two major thirds.

authentic cadence   A cadence in which the dominant chord (V) precedes the tonic (I).

bagatelle   A short, light composition, usually for piano.

bar or **bar line**   A vertical line through the staff to indicate a boundary for a measure of music.

Baroque period   The period in music history spanning approximately the years 1600–1750.

bass clef   The symbol 𝄢, which determines that the fourth line of the staff is F below middle C.

beat   The underlying pulse present in most music; the rhythmic unit to which one responds in marching or dancing.

beat groupings   See **meter**.

binary form   A musical design consisting of two sections, A and B, that contrast with each other.

bitonality   The use of two different keys simultaneously.

blue notes   Notes that are lowered—usually the third and the seventh tones of a major scale.

blues   Sorrow songs created by Black Americans that influenced the development of jazz. Special characteristics include flatted third and seventh scale tones, the use of groups of twelve measures, seventh chords, syncopation, and improvisation.

blues scale   A scale that can only be approximated in traditional notation or on the keyboard; a major scale with the third and the seventh pitches lowered a half step (the fifth is also lowered a half step in some bebop music).

boogie-woogie   A jazz piano style (fast blues) in which the left hand repeats a fast-moving bass (generally moving through tonic, subdominant, and dominant harmonies) while the right hand improvises a melody part.

bourrée   A popular dance of the Baroque period, in quick duple meter, with a short upbeat.

breve   A note value that is equivalent to two whole notes, written as ═ or н.

cadence   A point of arrival that punctuates a musical phrase, section, and composition.

canon   A contrapuntal composition in which all parts have the same melody throughout but start at different times. A round is a type of canon.

Celesta   A percussion instrument in the form of a small upright piano; its tone is produced by the striking of steel bars with hammers connected to a keyboard by a simplified piano action.

chorale   Hymn tune.

chord   A combination of three or more tones sounded together.

chord progression   A series of chords sounding in succession.

chord root   The pitch on which a chord is constructed.

chord tones   The individual pitches within a chord.

chromatic scale   A twelve-tone scale consisting entirely of half steps.

circle of fifths   The key signatures of the major and minor keys arranged in a circular sequence of perfect fifths.

classical music   A layman's term for art music of Western European civilization, usually created by a trained composer.

Classic period   The period in music history spanning approximately the years 1750–1820.

clavichord   A stringed keyboard instrument used from the fifteenth through the eighteenth centuries; instead of hammers striking the strings like on a piano, tangents (upright metal wedges) strike the strings.

clef   A symbol placed on a staff to designate a precise pitch that identifies the other pitches in the score.

compound meter   A grouping of beats (meter) in which the beat is divided into three equal parts.

Contemporary period   The period in Western music history spanning the twentieth century.

continuo   Abbreviation for basso continuo; the continuous bass part which was performed by the harpsichord or organ in works of the Baroque period and served as the basis for harmonies.

contour   The shape of a melodic line.

contrary motion   A type of motion in which two or more parts move in opposite directions.

damper pedal   The piano pedal to the far right, which, when pressed down, releases the dampers from the strings and allows the strings to vibrate freely, sustaining the sound; generally, used to produce a legato effect.

diatonic   A seven-tone scale, consisting of five whole steps and two half steps, utilizing every pitch name. Major and minor scales are diatonic scales.

diminished triad   A three-note chord built with two minor thirds.

dominant   The fifth degree of the scale; a chord constructed on the fifth degree of the scale.

dominant seventh chord   A four-note chord constructed on the fifth degree of the scale with a minor seventh added above the root.

double flat   A symbol that indicates that the written pitch is to be lowered two half steps: ♭♭.

double sharp   A symbol that indicates that the written pitch is to be raised two half steps: ×.

downbeat   The first beat of a measure (beat grouping), usually accented.

drone   An accompaniment created by sounding one or more tones (usually two, five notes apart) simultaneously and continuously throughout a composition or section of a composition; a special type of harmony.

duet   A composition written for two players.

duple meter   A grouping of beats (meter) into two ($\frac{2}{4}$, $\frac{2}{2}$).

duration   The length of time a musical tone sounds.

dynamics   The degree and range of loudness of musical sounds.

electronic music   Music made by creating, altering, and imitating sounds electronically. The basic tools of this kind of music are the tape recorder and the electronic synthesizer.

enharmonic tones   Tones sounding the same pitch but written differently, as E-flat and D-sharp.

étude   French word meaning "study"; a technical study designed to facilitate technique.

expressionism   A musical style of the early twentieth century in which irregular rhythms, jagged melody lines, and dissonances were used to express strong subjective feelings.

flat   A symbol that indicates that the written pitch is to be lowered a half step: ♭.

folk song   A song having no known composer, usually transmitted orally, and reflecting the musical consensus of a cultural group.

form   The plan, order, or design in which a piece of music is organized.

gavotte   A French dance in moderately quick duple meter, often with an upbeat of two quarter notes.

glissando   A very rapid sliding passage up or down the white and black keys.

grace note   A short note, printed in small type, that ornaments the note that follows it. A grace note is not counted in the rhythm of the measure.

grand or **great staff**   Treble and bass clef staves joined together by a vertical line and a bracket.

half step   The narrowest interval from one tone to another (in Western music); a semitone.

harmonic minor scale   A minor scale in which the pattern of whole and half steps is: whole, half, whole, whole, half, whole & half, half.

harmony   A simultaneous sounding of two or more tones.

harpsichord   A keyboard instrument, popular in the Renaissance and Baroque periods; instead of hammers striking the strings like on a piano, the strings are plucked by quills.

homophonic   A musical texture in which all parts move in the same rhythm but use different pitches, as in hymns; also, a melody supported by chords.

hymn   A religious song; usually a metric poem to be sung by a congregation.

imitation   The restatement of a theme in different voices (parts).

impressionism   A musical style of the late nineteenth and early twentieth centuries, in which musical textures and timbres were used to convey impressions (hint) rather than make precise "statements."

improvisation   Music performed extemporaneously, often within a framework determined by the musical style.

indeterminate music   "Chance" music emphasizing improvisation within limitations set by the composer.

interval   The distance between two tones, named by counting all pitch names involved; a harmonic interval occurs when two pitches are sounded simultaneously, and a melodic interval occurs when two pitches are sounded successively.

inversion   The rearrangement of the pitches of a chord, for example, CEG becomes GCE.

jazz   A style that originated with Black Americans in the early twentieth century, characterized by improvisation and syncopated rhythms.

key   The tonal raw materials of a composition, formed by the tonic and the notes related to the tonic. (Key may be said to be identical with scale.)

key signature   The sharps or the flats at the beginning of the staff, after the clef sign, indicating in which key or on what scale the composition is written.

leading tone   The seventh tone or triad of a major or a harmonic or melodic minor scale.

leger or **ledger lines** (LEH-jer)   Short lines above or below the five-line staff on which higher or lower pitches may be indicated.

major interval   An interval a half step larger than the corresponding minor interval.

major scale   A scale in which the pattern of whole and half steps is: whole, whole, half, whole, whole, whole, half.

major triad   A three-note chord with a major third and a minor third.

march   A composition written in duple meter with a strong, vigorous rhythm and regular phrases.

mazurka   A Polish dance in quick triple meter with strong emphasis on beat two or three.

measure   A unit of beats delineated by bar lines; informally called a "bar."

mediant   The third tone or triad of a major or minor scale.

Medieval period   Also called Middle Ages; the earliest period in Western music history, spanning approximately the years 500–1420.

melodic minor scale   A minor scale in which the ascending pattern of whole and half steps is: whole, half, whole, whole, whole, whole, half, whereas the descending pattern is identical with the natural minor scale.

melodic rhythm   Durations of pitches used in a melody.

melody   A succession of sounds (pitches) and silences moving one at a time through time.

meter   The grouping of beats in music.

meter signature   Two numerals that show the number of beats grouped in a measure and the basic beat: $\frac{3}{4}$.

middle C   The C midway between the treble and bass clefs; approximately midway on the piano keyboard.

minimalism A twentieth-century musical style in which the musical elements are subjected to a minimal amount of development; an attempt to simplify music by using the fewest of means.

minor interval An interval a half step smaller than the corresponding major interval.

minor scale A scale in which one characteristic feature is a half step between the second and third tones. There are three forms of minor scales: natural, harmonic, and melodic.

minor triad A three-note chord that includes a minor third and a major third.

minuet A dance in triple meter with an elegant, graceful quality of movement; of French origin.

modes Scales (each with seven notes) consisting of various patterns of whole and half steps. The seven possible modes—Ionian, Dorian, Phrygian, Lydian, Mixolydian, Aeolian, and Locrian—were used in the Medieval and Renaissance periods and served as the basis from which major and minor scales emerged.

modulation The change from one key to another within a composition.

monophonic A musical texture created when a single melody is heard without harmony.

motive A brief rhythmic or melodic figure that recurs throughout a composition as a unifying element.

musical style The characteristic manner in which the musical elements—melody, rhythm, harmony, and form—are treated in a piece of music.

natural A sign that cancels a sharp or a flat: ♮. A note that is neither sharp nor flat, as C, D, E, F, G, A, B on the piano keyboard.

natural minor scale A minor scale in which the pattern of whole and half steps is: whole, half, whole, whole, half, whole, whole.

neighboring tones Tones placed a step above (upper neighbor) or a step below (lower neighbor) two repeated pitches.

oblique motion A type of motion in which one part remains stationary while the other parts move.

octave The interval in which two pitches share the same letter name (C-C) and are eight steps apart (eight lines and spaces from one note to the next); one pitch with twice the frequency of the other.

opus (op.) A composition or group of compositions with designated numbers that indicate the chronological position of the composition(s) in the composer's total output.

organ A keyboard wind instrument consisting of a series of pipes standing on a wind chest; features one or more keyboards, operated by a player's hands and feet. The portative organ was a small portable organ of the late Middle Ages while the positive organ was a self-contained, medium-sized organ also used in the Middle Ages.

ostinato A continuous repetition of a melodic or rhythmic pattern.

parallel keys The major and minor scales that share the same tonic but have different key signatures.

parallel motion A type of motion in which two or more parts move in the same direction.

passing tones Tones placed stepwise between chord tones.

pattern *See* **motive.**

pedals Levers operated by the feet on pianos and organs; pianos have a damper pedal, a sostenuto pedal, and an una corda pedal.

pentatonic scale A five-tone scale often identified with the pattern of the black keys of the piano. Many other five-tone arrangements are possible.

phrase A musical segment with a clear beginning and ending, comparable to a simple sentence or a clause in speech.

plagal cadence A cadence in which the subdominant chord (IV) precedes the tonic (I).

polyphonic A musical texture created when two or more melodies sound simultaneously.

polytonal Music that employs two or more tonalities (or keys) simultaneously.

prelude An introductory piece for a larger composition or drama, usually written for a solo instrument; in the nineteenth century "Prelude" was used as the title for piano character pieces.

primary chords The three chords built on the first degree (I), the fourth degree (IV), and the fifth degree (V) of any major or harmonic or melodic minor scale.

quadruple meter A grouping of beats into four ($\frac{4}{4}$, $\frac{4}{8}$, $\frac{4}{2}$).

ragtime Piano music, developed at the turn of the century, that features a syncopated melody against a steady "oom PAH" bass; piano "rags" are usually divided into three or four different sections—each symmetrical in length.

relative keys The major and minor scales that share the same key signature but different tonics.

Renaissance period The period in Western music history spanning approximately the years 1420–1600.

rest A symbol designating silence.

retrograde Backward motion; beginning with the last note of a melody and ending with the first.

rhythm All of the duration or lengths of sounds and silences that occur in music; the organization of sounds and silences in time.

rhythm of the melody *See* **melodic rhythm.**

rhythm pattern Any grouping, generally brief, of long and short sounds and silences.

Romantic period The period in Western music history spanning approximately the years 1820–1900.

rondo A musical form consisting of a recurring section with two or more contrasting sections, as A B A C A.

root The tone on which a chord is built. A chord using C as its root is labeled a C chord.

round A melody performed by two or more groups entering at stated and different times.

scale A pattern of pitches arranged in ascending or descending order. Scales are identified by their specific arrangement of whole and half steps. *See also* **major scale; minor scale; chromatic scale; pentatonic scale; whole-tone scale.**

secondary chords The four chords built on the second degree (II), the third degree (III), the sixth degree (VI), and the seventh degree (VII) of any major or harmonic or melodic minor scale.

section A distinct portion of a composition; one of a number of parts that together make a composition. A section consists of several phrases.

serial music   General term for twentieth-century compositions that are based on new rules and principles rather than on the traditional rules of melody and harmony.

seventh chord   A four-note chord built in thirds.

sharp   A symbol that raises the pitch a half step (♯).

shifting meter   The changing of beat groupings in music, as from twos to threes.

simple meter   A grouping of beats (meter) in which the beat is divided into two equal parts.

skip   A melodic interval exceeding a second or whole step.

slur   A curved line, above or below a number of notes, that indicates that these pitches should be connected (legato).

sonata   An extended composition in several movements for one to two instruments.

sonata form   The most important form of the Classic period; includes a main theme and a subsidiary theme presented in the *exposition*, followed by a *development* of the themes, and concludes with a restatement, or *recapitulation*, of the themes.

sostenuto pedal   The piano pedal in the middle, which, when depressed, sustains only those tones whose dampers are already raised by the action of the keys.

step   An interval of a second, as A to B.

subdominant   The fourth degree of the scale; a chord constructed on the fourth degree of the scale.

submediant   The sixth tone or triad of a major or minor scale.

subtonic   The seventh tone of a natural minor scale.

supertonic   The second tone or triad of a major or minor scale.

syncopation   Placement of emphasis on normally weak beats or weak parts of beats.

tempo   The rate of speed of music.

ternary form   A musical design consisting of three sections, A B A; two are the same and the middle one is different.

tetrachord   Four successive scale tones.

theme   A distinctive melodic statement, usually part of a long movement.

theme and variations   A composition in which each section is a modified version of the original musical theme.

tie   A curved line that connects two identical notes and indicates that they should be performed as a single note; to perform, strike the first note only and hold through the time value of the second:

timbre   The quality or color of sound; the characteristic sound of an instrument. Synonyms: tone color, tone quality.

time   Commonly used in place of more precise terms, namely, meter, rhythm, tempo, duration.

time signature   *See* **meter signature.**

tonality   The relationship of tones in a scale to the tonic.

tonal music   Music that is centered on a particular tonic or key center.

tone cluster   The simultaneous sounding of a group of adjacent tones, usually dissonant in sound.

tone row   A series of twelve tones (the tones of a chromatic scale), arranged in a specific order by the composer.

tonic   The central tone of the key and the first note of the scale.

transposition   Changing a piece of music from one key to another.

treble clef   The symbol 𝄞, which determines the second line of the staff as G above middle C.

triad   A three-note chord with pitches a third apart.

triple meter   A grouping of beats (meter) into threes ($\frac{3}{4}$, $\frac{3}{8}$, $\frac{3}{2}$).

twelve-tone row   *See* **tone row.**

una corda pedal   The piano pedal to the far left, which, when depressed, shifts the grand piano keyboard so that each hammer strikes only two of the three strings in the upper register and only one in the lower; the same effect of reducing the volume is achieved by different means on an upright piano.

upbeat   *See* **anacrusis.**

virginal   A small type of harpsichord with one set of strings and jacks and one keyboard; the earliest forms were shaped like a rectangular box and placed on a table or held in the performer's lap.

Western art music   Art music of Western European civilization, usually created by a trained composer.

whole step   An interval comprising two consecutive half steps, as C to D.

whole-tone scale   A scale of six different tones, each a whole step apart.

Ensemble Pieces

Technique Exercises

Rhythm Exercises

Composing Projects

Index of Musical Selections
(alphabetized by title)

[*Ensemble pieces are indicated in* **boldface**]

Subject Index

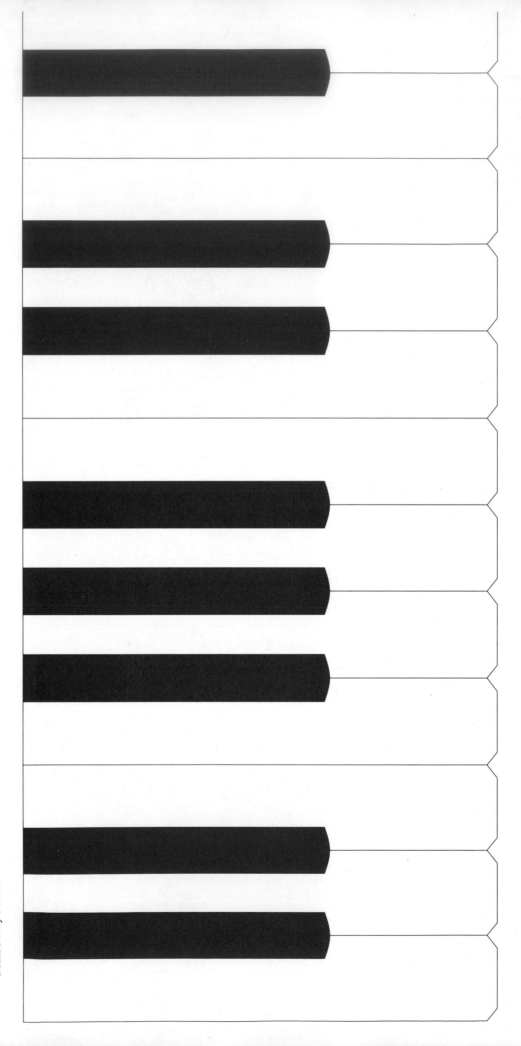

Piano keyboard

Your head start to making beautiful music

Written specifically for students in a group or class environment, this popular book helps you feel comfortable with the piano and the music—right from the start. With Carolynn A. Lindeman's step-by-step guidance, in no time you will experience the excitement of performing your first piece of music.

PianoLab offers simultaneous development of music reading and playing skills with interesting technique exercises and a wonderful repertoire of the music you've always wanted to play. Musical concepts are covered in every chapter and are applied through performance, analysis, improvisation, transposition, harmonization, and composition.

This Second Edition also contains:

- Playing excerpts from such popular pieces as Lennon/McCartney's "With a Little Help from My Friends," Led Zeppelin's "Stairway to Heaven," "Memory" from Andrew Lloyd Weber's *Cats*, three new jazz ensemble pieces from Lee Evans's "Razzle Dazzle" and "Jazzmatazz," and much more

- Timelines of Western art music and history and of selected keyboard composers and instruments

- Biographical sketches of composers discussed in the book

About the author

Carolynn A. Lindeman (D.M.A., Stanford University) is Professor of Music at San Francisco State University and Coordinator of Music Education. President of the California Music Educators Association (1990–1992), Dr. Lindeman is a frequent clinician at national and international conferences. In addition to *PianoLab*, she has written *Women Composers of Ragtime* and has coauthored *The Musical Classroom: Backgrounds, Models, and Skills for Elementary Teaching* and *MusicLab: An Introduction to Music Fundamentals*.

ISBN 0-534-13944-2

9 780534 139445

90000